Rich Brott

How to Receive

PROSPERITY
&
PROVISION

17 Biblical Principles
You Must Know

Published by

ABC Book Publishing

AbcBookPublishing.com
Printed in U.S.A.

How to Receive Prosperity & Provision
17 Biblical Principles You Must Know

All scripture quotations, unless otherwise indicated, are taken from the *Holy Bible, New International Version*. *NIV*. Copyright © 1973, 1978, 1984 by International Bible Society. Used by permission of Zondervan Publishing House. All rights reserved.

Other Versions used are:

AMP- Amplified Bible.

Amer. Std.-American Standard Version, 1901.

KJV-King James Version. Authorized King James Version.

NASB-Scripture taken from the *New American Standard Bible*, ©1960, 1962, 1963, 1968, 1971, 1972, 1973, 1975, 1977 by The Lockman Foundation. Used by permission.

Scripture taken from the *New King James Version*. Copyright © 1979, 1980, 1982 by Thomas Nelson, Inc. Publishers. Used by permission. All rights reserved.

Verses marked (*TLB*) are taken from *The Living Bible* © 1971. Used by permission of Tyndale House Publishers, Inc., Wheaton, IL 60189. All rights reserved.

Scripture taken from *THE MESSAGE: The Bible in Contemporary Language* © 2002 by Eugene H. Peterson. All rights reserved.

This publication is designed to provide interesting reading material and general information with regard to the subject matter covered. It is printed, distributed and sold with the understanding that neither the publisher nor the author is engaged in rendering religious, family, legal, accounting, business, investing, financial, credit, debt or other professional advice. If any such advice is required, the services of a competent professional person should be sought. In summary, the content contained herein is not given as advice, rather it is strictly for the purpose of your reading entertainment.

Every effort has been made to supply complete and accurate information. However, neither the publisher nor the author assumes any responsibility for its use, nor for any infringements of patents or other rights of third parties that would result.

First Edition, January 1, 2008
Richard A. Brott

About the Author

Rich Brott holds a Bachelor of Science degree in Business and Economics and a Master of Business Administration.

Rich has served in an executive position of some very successful businesses. He has functioned on the board of directors for churches, businesses, and charities and served on a college advisory board. Rich has traveled to more than 25 countries on teaching assignments and business concerns.

He has authored thirty-five books including:

- *5 Simple Keys to Financial Freedom*
- *10 Life-Changing Attitudes That Will Make You a Financial Success*
- *15 Biblical Responsibilities Leading to Financial Wisdom*
- *30 Biblical Principles for Managing Your Money*
- *35 Keys to Financial Independence*
- *A Biblical Perspective On Giving Generously*
- *A Biblical Perspective On Tithing Faithfully*
- *A Biblical Perspective On Tithing & Giving*
- *Achieving Financial Alignment*
- *Activating Your Personal Faith to Receive*
- *All the Financial Scriptures in the Bible*
- *Basic Principles for Business Success*
- *Basic Principles for Developing Personal and Business Vision*
- *Basic Principles for Managing a Successful Business*
- *Basic Principles for Maximizing Your Personal Cash Flow*
- *Basic Principles for Starting a Successful Business*
- *Basic Principles of Conservative Investing*

- *Biblical Principles for Achieving Personal Success*
- *Biblical Principles for Becoming Debt Free*
- *Biblical Principles for Building a Successful Business*
- *Biblical Principles for Financial Success - Student Workbook*
- *Biblical Principles for Financial Success - Teacher Workbook*
- *Biblical Principles for Personal Evangelism*
- *Biblical Principles for Releasing Financial Provision*
- *Biblical Principles for Staying Out of Debt*
- *Biblical Principles for Success in Personal Finance*
- *Biblical Principles That Create Success Through Productivity*
- *Business, Occupations, Professions & Vocations In the Bible*
- *Family Finance Handbook*
- *Family Finance Student Workbook*
- *Family Finance Teacher Workbook*
- *How To Receive Prosperity & Provision*
- *Prosperity Has a Purpose*
- *Public Relations for the Local Church*
- *Successful Time Management*

He and his wife Karen, have been married for 36 years. Rich Brott resides in Portland, Oregon, with his wife, three children, son-in-law and granddaughter.

Dedication

I dedicate this book to those who seek the complete fulfillment of all of God's promises over their lives.

Table of Contents

Introduction

Psalms 20:4

May He grant you according to your heart's desire, And fulfill all your purpose. NKJV

3 John 2

Beloved, I pray that you may prosper in all things and be in health, just as your soul prospers. NKJV

Proverbs 28:25

A greedy man stirs up dissension, but he who trusts in the LORD will prosper.

Proverbs 11:25

A generous man will prosper; he who refreshes others will himself be refreshed.

Jeremiah 29:11

For I know the plans I have for you," declares the LORD, "plans to prosper you and not to harm you, plans to give you hope and a future.

Let's begin with the fact that God wants to provide good things to His children. He wants for you to prosper and be successful in your God given gifts and callings. But God is no vending machine, nor does His promises come without conditions. The principles upon which a person builds his/her financial future are very important. They can ensure security in the later years of a person's life.

The manner in which finances are acquired and disbursed must be based on sound moral guidelines. Desire for money can become an obsession. When it does, nothing can satisfy. Peace of mind is gone. The joy of a new day gives way to worry about retaining what one has and gaining more and more.

If God cannot trust you with a hundred dollars now, how can He trust you with a thousand or a hundred thousand? Christians have access to unlimited and unimaginable resources. But with this access comes accountability. This is a lot of trust that God places in our lives. It is more than just finances. It is our entire life and how we handle it with faithfulness, responsibility, accountability, honesty, and integrity.

Learn to Receive the Prosperity and Provision of God!

Rich Brott

Principle 1

The Principle of
Enjoying All Things

1 Timothy 6:17

Charge them that are rich in this world, that they be not highminded, nor trust in uncertain riches, but in the living God, who giveth us richly all things to enjoy. (kjv)

Some people have the wrong idea of wealth, relegating it only to dollar signs and a huge bank account. But true riches are very different than you might think. Having good health and the ability to enjoy one's family, friends, and life in general is what real wealth is all about. God wants us to be happy and enjoy His creation. The following story better demonstrates what this principle is all about.

One day a very rich father took his family on a trip to the country. "How come we're doing this, Dad?" one of the kids wanted to know. "Oh," he replied, "I just want to show you how poor some people can be." So they spent a day and a night at the farm of a very poor family. When they returned from their journey, the father asked his son, "Well, how did you enjoy that?" The young man said, "Aw, it was super, Dad! Thanks!" "And...what did you learn?" the father asked. And his boy answered, "I saw that we have a dog here at home...but that farmer and his family had FOUR dogs. We have a swimming pool that reaches to the middle of the garden; but they have a creek that doesn't even have an end. We have imported lamps in our garden; but they have the stars they can see every night. Our patio reaches to the front yard, but they have a whole horizon.

The boy stopped for a moment and looked at his shaken father. "Dad," he said, "you told me you were going to show me how poor people can be. I get it—we're really poor, aren't we?"

Principle 2

The Principle of Abundant Blessing

Malachi 3:10–11

> *"Bring all the tithes into the storehouse so that there will be food enough in my Temple; if you do, I will open up the windows of heaven for you and pour out a blessing so great you won't have room enough to take it in! Try it! Let me prove it to you! Your crops will be large, for I will guard them from insects and plagues. Your grapes won't shrivel away before they ripen," says the Lord Almighty.* (tlb)

Sometimes we don't realize how blessed we are. We think in terms of new cars, clothes, furniture, the size of our house, the size of our bank account, etc. But when this Scripture talks about opening up the windows of heaven and pouring out a great blessing, don't forget all the wonderful ways in which you have become the recipient of His love and blessing. In this story of a rich landowner and one of his tenant farmers, we see who was the real rich person:

A rich landowner named Carl often rode around his vast estate so he could congratulate himself on his great wealth. One day, while riding around his estate on his favorite horse, he saw Hans, an old tenant farmer. Hans was sitting under a tree when Carl rode by. Hans said, "I was just thanking God for my food." Carl protested, "If that is all I had to eat, I wouldn't feel like giving thanks." Hans replied, "God has given me everything I need, and I am thankful for it."

The old farmer added, "It is strange you should come by today because I had a dream last night. In my dream a voice told me, 'The richest man in the valley will die tonight.' I don't know what it means, but I thought I ought to tell you." Carl snorted. "Dreams are nonsense." He galloped away, but he could not forget Hans's words: "The richest man in the valley will die tonight."

He was obviously the richest man in the valley, so he invited his doctor to his house that evening. Carl told the doctor what Hans had said. After a thorough examination, the doctor told the wealthy landowner, "Carl, you are as strong and healthy as a horse. There is no way you are going to die tonight."

Nevertheless, for assurance, the doctor stayed with Carl, and they played cards through the night. The doctor left the next morning, and Carl apologized for becoming so upset over the old man's dream. At about nine o'clock, a messenger arrived at Carl's door. "What is it?" Carl demanded. The messenger explained, "It's about old Hans. He died last night in his sleep."

Principle 3

The Principle of Continual Protection

Malachi 3:11–12

> *"I will prevent pests from devouring your crops, and the vines in your fields will not cast their fruit," says the Lord Almighty.*

John Edmund Haggai tells the following story of his father's faithful tithing and giving nature and of God's continual protection upon his family.

One winter morning in 1931, I came down to breakfast—and found the table empty.

It was cold outside. The worst blizzard on record had paralyzed the city. No cars were out. The snow had drifted up two stories high against our house, blackening the windows.

"Daddy, what's happening?" I asked. I was six years old. Gently Dad told me our fuel and food supplies were exhausted. He'd just put the last piece of coal on the fire. Mother had eight ounces of milk left for my baby brother Tom. After that—nothing.

"So what are we going to eat?" I asked. "We'll have our devotions first, John Edmund," he said, in a voice that told me I should not ask questions.

My father was a pastor. As a Christian he'd been chased out of his Syrian homeland. He arrived as a teenager in the United States with no money and barely a word of English—nothing but his vocation to preach. He knew hardship of a kind few see today. Yet my parents consistently gave away at least 10 percent of their income, and no one but God ever knew when we were in financial need.

That morning, Dad read the Scriptures as usual, and afterwards we knelt for prayer. He prayed earnestly for the family, for our relatives and friends, for those he called the "missionaries of the cross" and those in the city who'd endured the blizzard without adequate shelter. Then he prayed something like this: "Lord, Thou knowest we have no more coal to burn. If it can please Thee, send us some fuel. If not, Thy will be done—we thank Thee for warm clothes and bed covers, which will keep us comfortable, even without the fire. Also, Thou knowest we have no food except milk for Baby Thomas. If it can please Thee…" For someone facing bitter cold and hunger, he was remarkably calm. Nothing deflected him from completing the family devotions—not even the clamor we now heard beyond the muffling wall of snow.

Finally someone pounded on the door. The visitor had cleared the snow off the windowpane, and we saw his face peering in. "Your door's iced up," he yelled. "I can't open it." The devotions over, Dad jumped up. He pulled; the man pushed. When the door suddenly gave, an avalanche of snow fell into the entrance hall. I didn't recognize the man, and I don't think Dad did either because he said politely, "Can I help you?"

The man explained he was a farmer who'd heard Dad preach in Allegan three years earlier. "I awakened at four o'clock this morning," he said, "and I couldn't get you out of my mind. The truck was stuck in the garage, so I harnessed the horses to the sleigh and came over."

"Well, please come in," my father said. On any other occasion, he'd have added, "And have some breakfast with us." But, of course, today there was no breakfast. The man thanked him. And then—to our astonishment—he plucked a large box off the sleigh. More than sixty years later, I can see that box as clear as yesterday. It contained milk, eggs, butter, pork chops, grain, homemade bread, and a host of other things. When the farmer had delivered the box, he went back out and got a cord of wood. Finally, after a very hearty breakfast, he insisted Dad take a ten-dollar bill.

Almost every day Dad reminded us that "God is the Provider." And my experience throughout adult life has confirmed it. "I have never seen the righteous forsaken nor their children begging bread" (Psalm 37:25). The Bible said it. But Dad and Mom showed me it was true.

Principle 4

The Principle of Enlarged Measure

Luke 6:38

> *"Give, and it will be given to you. A good measure, pressed down, shaken together and running over, will be poured into your lap. For with the measure you use, it will be measured to you."*

Note that selflessness is the theme of this Scripture. In short, the principle of enlarged measure is this: We must give if we ever hope to have a return. Second, the size of our return is dependent upon the size of our gift. Third, our return will be bountiful; over and above our expectations. In short, when I hoard my money and keep it all to myself, that's all I have. It never increases, but there is a huge opportunity for it to decrease. However, when I give it away, God multiplies it. Some people want to tell God that they expect Him to not only meet their needs, but to also supply them with their wants. And only then will they consider giving something away. But I am so sorry—it does not work that way. God's way is that you give first, and then He pours out the blessing. And not only that, the measure of blessing is dependent upon the measure of your gift.

Money CAN Buy Happiness

Let me give you a possible scenario for buying personal happiness. What if your total income were fifty thousand dollars a year? And let's agree that you are by now a faithful and obedient tithe payer (i.e. you give God 10 percent of your increase and you have become a good steward of the 90 percent He has entrusted you with). Obviously, if you are a good manager, you are already living comfortably below the 90 percent remainder. Now let's suppose that you work for someone else and you receive a five-thousand-dollar raise in your annual income. What should you do with that? Should you buy a newer car? How about take a longer vacation? Maybe you could buy more "stuff" so that you need a bigger garage or a larger shed to store it in.

Consider the "happiness" alternative. Instead of using the money to heap new "stuff" upon yourself, why not use the additional increase to help others? Here are a few ideas for you:

$ 5,000   **Increase in Personal Income**

<$ 500>   additional tithe to your local church

<$1,200>   support a missionary $100 per month

<$ 500>   support a homeless shelter

<$ 300>   pay some utility bills of an unemployed person

<$ 500>   donate to a food program for the needy

<$ 500>   arrange for a poor family to enjoy a nice Christmas

<$1,000>   help a college student with tuition and/or books

<$ 400>   buy new tires for an older person on a fixed income

<$ 100>   give to a neighbor child to help with summer camp

$ 0   **Balance of Increase**

Try this one time with your increase, and just see whether or not you receive more joy and happiness then you've ever experienced before. Honor the Lord with your increase; honor the Lord with your wealth. The principle of enlarged measure begins with the gift of giving.

Principle 5

The Principle of Forward Thinking

S upernatural prosperity and provision works hand-in-hand with personal prosperity and provision. What are you doing to prepare yourself in a way that God can bless? Planning ahead for an eventual result provides a road map to follow with predesignated milestones. If you don't have a plan, how will you know when you are successful? Without a predetermined road map, how do you know where you are going? Without a target in your crosshair, how will you know if you are pointed in the right direction?

Planning for the future is biblical. Joseph told the people of Egypt to prepare for the coming famine. During the years of surplus, Joseph was wise enough to gather the excess and store it for later use. He was a great model of advance preparation in process. The preparation done by the Egyptians cared for their needs during the years of lack.

Genesis 41:48–49

> *Joseph collected all the food produced in those seven years of abundance in Egypt and stored it in the cities. In each city he put the food grown in the fields surrounding it. Joseph stored up huge quantities of grain, like the*

sand of the sea; it was so much that he stopped keeping records because it was beyond measure.

While we are in good health, we too have the opportunity to be employed and should be living below our means. We should be setting aside money to help should there be a time of financial drought in our lives. We should be living the principle of advance preparation and planning.

Here is a biblical story about a man about to lose his job planning ahead for his future well-being, even though he does so in an unscrupulous way:

Luke 16:1–8

Jesus told his disciples: "There was a rich man whose manager was accused of wasting his possessions. So he called him in and asked him, 'What is this I hear about you? Give an account of your management, because you cannot be manager any longer.' The manager said to himself, What shall I do now? My master is taking away my job. I'm not strong enough to dig, and I'm ashamed to beg—I know what I'll do so that, when I lose my job here, people will welcome me into their houses. So he called in each one of his master's debtors. He asked the first, 'How much do you owe my master?' 'Eight hundred gallons of olive oil,' he replied. The manager told him, 'Take your bill, sit down quickly, and make it four hundred.' Then he asked the second, 'And how much do you owe?' 'A thousand bushels of wheat,' he replied. He told him, 'Take your bill and make it eight hundred.' The master commended the dishonest manager because he had acted shrewdly. For the people of this world are more shrewd in dealing with their own kind than are the people of the light."

Sensible people look ahead and plan for the future. They manage money to provide benefit for the present, as well as the future. Christ is suggesting that in doing good works, we should consider our future with just as much ingenuity as the dishonest steward considered his future. As stewards of Jesus Christ, we are mandated with a responsibility to use every means at our disposal to spread the Good News to all. In doing so, our gains will have great effect in eternal matters.

The shrewdness with which the unjust servant negated his responsibility to his lord was commended. He promoted his cause with the utmost care and effort. With an unprincipled passion, he sought to use his master's money in securing advantage after his inevitable dismissal. Christ was simply asking those to whom he spoke to be just as inventive, but for a better cause. This can happen only when we look down the line a bit and seek to plan ahead. The message is clear: In our stewardship responsibility to God, we should be at least as wholehearted and energetic as the misguided steward was in prosecuting his own interests.

Principle 6

The Principle of Finding God's Provision

Matthew 17:27

"But so that we may not offend them, go to the lake and throw out your line. Take the first fish you catch; open its mouth and you will find a four-drachma coin. Take it and give it to them for my tax and yours."

When did you last go searching for the favor of God? There are plenty of Scriptures that talk about asking God and seeking Him with our whole heart—all of our heart—100 percent, not just a small part.

Psalm 119:58

I entreated Your favor with my whole heart; Be merciful to me according to Your word. (nkjv)

When we seek supernatural provision from heaven, we must ask for divine favor. When in need, many simply reach for the worn-out charge card and incur more personal debt without giving God a chance to provide for their needs. Before you pay for it, be sure to pray for it.

James 4:2

"You do not have, because you do not ask God."

Sometimes we don't receive from God only because we fail to ask. Take time to pause in all of the numerous activities of your daily schedule to simply "ask." When you keep your mouth shut, He keeps the storehouse door closed.

Matthew 7:7–12

"Ask and it will be given to you; seek and you will find; knock and the door will be opened to you. For everyone who asks receives; he who seeks finds; and to him who knocks, the door will be opened. Which of you, if his son asks for bread, will give him a stone? Or if he asks for a fish, will give him a snake? If you, then, though you are evil, know how to give good gifts to your children, how much more will your Father in heaven give good gifts to those who ask him!"

Notice the order here: Ask, Seek, Knock. Combine these into an acronym and you get this: ASK. The bottom line? You don't have because you don't ask.

Principle 7

The Principle of Just-In-Time Provision

Matthew 17:26

> *"So go down to the shore and throw in a line, and open the mouth of the first fish you catch. You will find a coin to cover the taxes for both of us; take it and pay them."* (tlb)

One of the wonderful principles of the Bible is that of divine supply—God promises to supply our every need. Financial supply is a God-given gift. God gives us many gifts, but His greatest gift was His death on the cross, providing a living sacrifice for our sins. He has given us the gift of salvation. He gives us the gift of life, family, friends, and good health. The Bible says that He loves to give us good gifts.

Matthew 7:11

> *"If you, then, though you are evil, know how to give good gifts to your children, how much more will your Father in heaven give good gifts to those who ask him!"*

If a gift is promised but not yet given, why do some people borrow and go into debt just to obtain what God had intended to supply anyway? Is this because of our impatience or a lack of trust? Is it because we don't really have faith for God's abundant supply or don't agree with His timetable?

When two people marry in the traditional Christian wedding, the vow includes the statement "Until death do us part." Many good marriages break apart because of a great wall of financial miscommunication. Unfortunately, in our current culture this sacred vow might be more accurate if it said, "Until debt do us part." Many statistics now conclude that the majority of all divorces are influenced by financial controversy and seemingly insurmountable debt.

God knows your need.

He wants to provide for you.

He desires to bless you with good gifts.

Everything we have is a gift from the Lord. He desires to bless and prosper us. Jeremiah 29:11 says, "For I know the plans I have for you," declares the Lord, "plans to prosper you and not to harm you, plans to give you hope and a future."

Along with these gifts come personal responsibility. Jesus talked about stewardship a great deal. *Jesus dealt with money matters, because money matters!*

Both Jesus and Satan know that "where your treasure is, there your heart will be also" (Matthew 6:21). That's why both are very interested in what we do with our money. *Our attitude toward money is a spiritual matter!* If our attitude is right, we will be good stewards of all God has allowed us to oversee, and when we do so, an unending supply of provision will come our way.

Principle 8

The Principle of
No Worry

Matthew 6:34

> *"Therefore do not worry about tomorrow, for tomorrow will worry about itself. Each day has enough trouble of its own."*

A song I learned in Sunday school was "Why Worry When You Can Pray?" Although I sang it in Sunday school, we ought to be singing it, or at least following its advice, as mature adults.

This Scripture reminds us that He will provide us with plenty of food:

Acts 14:17

> *He provides you with plenty of food and fills your hearts with joy.*

Psalm 37:25

> *I was young and now I am old, yet I have never seen the righteous forsaken or their children begging bread.*

Worry is the opposite of faith. A Christian cannot be filled with faith and worry at the same time. The psalmist David had plenty of times when he could have been filled with worry…even to the point of wondering if his enemies would kill him. Even Jesus taught us to ask for our *daily* bread. He is more than willing to provide for us, but apparently is very adamant that we ask for his help first. God never abandons His children. He always provides for them. In His time, God will always right the wrongs, avenge injustice, and keep His promises.

God will provide for you through many natural resources available to Him. In addition to the ongoing natural resources He has placed on the earth, when desirable, He will provide for us through supernatural means. He fed the prophet Elijah with food sent by ravens. He fed the five thousand men (plus women and children) from a few meager morsels of food. When we were children, we never worried about our parents providing for us. My parents provided me with a warm bed, daily food, and a roof over my head. Nothing was left to chance. In this manner, our heavenly Father provides for our needs daily. Day after day, month after month, He proves His love for us, even knowing our needs before we ask Him.

Matthew 6:8

"Do not be like them, for your Father knows what you need before you ask him."

1 Peter 5:7

Cast all your anxiety on him because he cares for you.

Psalm 37:3–5

Trust in the Lord and do good; dwell in the land and enjoy safe pasture. Delight yourself in the Lord and he will give you the desires of your heart. Commit your way to the Lord; trust in him and he will do this.

Psalm 115:12

The Lord remembers us and will bless us.

Proverbs 3:5

Trust in the Lord with all your heart and lean not on your own understanding.

Jesus compares our need for faith and trust in Him and suggests that we learn a lesson from the birds. The birds are not lazy by any means: they search for food, dig their worms, snatch bugs, build nests, work hard, and are very productive. Yet the Scripture says that it is God that feeds them.

Matthew 6:26–27

"Look at the birds of the air; they do not sow or reap or store away in barns, and yet your heavenly Father feeds them. Are you not much more valuable than they? Who of you by worrying can add a single hour to his life?"

This is a story told about a man who had a need. It is a rather fun tale, whether true or not:

There once was a man who had nothing for his family to eat. He had an old shotgun and three bullets. So he decided that he would go out and kill something for dinner.

As he went down the road, he saw a rabbit. He shot at the rabbit and missed it. Then he saw a squirrel and fired a shot at the squirrel and missed it. As he went further, he saw a wild turkey in the tree. He had only one bullet, but a voice came to him and said, "Pray first, aim high, and stay focused."

However, at the same time he saw a deer, which was a better kill. He brought the gun down and aimed at the deer. But then he saw a rattlesnake between his legs about to bite him, so he naturally brought the gun down further to shoot the rattlesnake.

Still, the voice said again to him, "I said, 'Pray, aim high, and stay focused.'" So the man decided to listen to the voice. He prayed, then aimed the gun high up in the tree and shot the wild turkey. The bullet bounced off the turkey and killed the deer. The handle fell off the gun and hit the snake in the head and killed it. And when the gun had gone off, it knocked the man into a pond. When he stood to look around, he had fish in all his pockets, a dead deer, and a turkey to eat.

Matthew 6:28–31

> *"And why do you worry about clothes? See how the lilies of the field grow. They do not labor or spin. Yet I tell you that not even Solomon in all his splendor was dressed like one of these. If that is how God clothes the grass of the field, which is here today and tomorrow is thrown into the fire, will he not much more clothe you, O you of little faith? So do not worry, saying, 'What shall we eat?' or 'What shall we drink?' or 'What shall we wear?'"*

In the above verse, Jesus has each of us take a look at the flowers of the field.

Matthew 6:27

"Who of you by worrying can add a single hour to his life?"

Then finally Jesus sums up the entire address on the subject of worry by showing us the futility of spending time with worry.

Why worry when you can pray? Worry about nothing; pray about everything!

Principle 9

The Principle of
Open Floodgates

Malachi 3:10

"Test me in this," says the Lord Almighty, "and see if I will not throw open the floodgates of heaven."

The dictionary defines reciprocity as a relation of mutual dependence or action or influence. In my opinion, this Scripture is talking about a biblical law of divine reciprocity. We give in obedience to the Word of God, and then God gives to us in return. We plant the seed, we water it with obedience to all of God's principles, and we yield a harvest.

Growing up in a preacher's home, I often saw my dad make house visits to local businesspeople who asked for prayer and sought after the favor of God. They did so with their giving, first of their tithes, then with their offerings. Yet some of them never darkened the doors of the church. These people of the business world knew the principle of open floodgates and open heavens even though they were not church members. It is a universal biblical law. The Lord Almighty even challenges us to "test" Him to see if it really works.

Deuteronomy 28:11–14

The Lord will grant you abundant prosperity—in the fruit of your womb, the young of your livestock and the crops of your ground—in the land he swore to your forefathers to give you. The Lord will open the heavens, the storehouse of his bounty, to send rain on your land in season and to bless all the work of your hands. You will lend to many nations but will borrow from none. The Lord will make you the head, not the tail. If you pay attention to the commands of the Lord your God that I give you this day and carefully follow them, you will always be at the top, never at the bottom.

Principle 10

The Principle of
Open Windows

Deuteronomy 28:12

> *"The Lord will open the heavens, the storehouse of his bounty, to send rain on your land in season and to bless all the work of your hands. You will lend to many nations but will borrow from none."*

One way God opens the windows of heaven is by keeping us from untold financial disasters.

Malachi 3:10–11 says:

> *Bring ye all the tithes into the storehouse, that there may be meat in mine house, and prove me now herewith, saith the Lord of hosts, if I will not open you the windows of heaven, and pour you out a blessing, that there shall not be room enough to receive it. And I will rebuke the devourer for your sakes, and he shall not destroy the fruits of your ground; neither shall your vine cast her fruit before the time in the field, saith the Lord of hosts. (kjv)*

What does it mean to "rebuke the devourer"? Many things create havoc in our financial lives. It may be the loss of a job, auto repairs, home maintenance, or medical bills. From time to time, all of us experience difficulty in this regard. And when "out of nowhere" expenses come, they can be burdensome and costly.

However, what we don't know is all that God keeps away from us. The Bible says that when we are faithful in our giving, our crops will be large and God will keep the insects and plagues away. No matter what kind of "crop" you're planting, God is working on your behalf.

Yet another way God opens the windows of heaven is by blessing us when we give. Generosity is God's antidote to greed. The heart and attitude of a blessed person is worth looking at. After all, don't we all want to be blessed people? Blessed people are set apart in many ways because they have learned how to be blessed. We all have the opportunity to receive the blessing of God and be "under the shadow of the Almighty" (Psalm 91:1). The blessed person gives of his or her resources freely, cheerfully, and out of genuine appreciation to God.

When we look upon the attitudes and heart of a blessed person, what will we discover? What is the heart like? What kind of attitude does one need to receive the blessing? What about the heart of a blessed person? What theme was so important to Jesus that He talked about it more than anything else? Was it heaven? Was it repentance? Was it prayer? Was it salvation? No. It was the subject of money. He knew that if He had our money, He would certainly have our hearts.

What about the attitude of a blessed person? Overall, the principal attitude must be that all money and possessions belong to God. He trusts us with the care of these things until we prove ourselves unworthy of His trust. It's not our money, so it's not our problem to worry about it. It is our basic responsibility as good stewards to use it correctly.

Principle 11

The Principle of Overflowing Barns

Proverbs 3:10

Then your barns will be filled to overflowing, and your vats will brim over with new wine.

This is a wonderful promise, the principle of overflowing barns. It is for everyone who meets the condition that precedes the agreement. The conditions to this guarantee are twofold. First, you are to honor God with your possessions. Second, you are to give the first-fruits of all of your increase. A great principle, which is wrapped by a wonderful promise. Let's see what it all means.

How do we honor the Lord? Today when we honor others, we may do so at banquets or special dinners in their honor, or we may give them a plaque or special award for their accomplishments, or we may honor a friend by sending a card and gift. Graduates are honored with public recognition and newlyweds are honored with a reception. We honor God by making sure that He holds first place in our lives. We make sure that in the giving of our time, money, trust, and prayers, He knows that our hearts are set upon Him. We place Him as Lord of our life by doing so. We honor Him with hearts full of gratitude because of His abundant blessing in our life.

Proverbs 10:22

The blessing of the Lord brings wealth, and he adds no trouble to it.

Some of the happiest people on earth are those who give generously. On the other hand, some of the most miserable people today are those who cling to every last dime and never use their prosperity to bless others.

Proverbs 11:25–28

> *The one who blesses others is abundantly blessed; those who help others are helped. Curses on those who drive a hard bargain! Blessings on all who play fair and square! The one who seeks good finds delight; the student of evil becomes evil. A life devoted to things is a dead life, a stump; a God-shaped life is a flourishing tree. (The Message)*

Principle 12

The Principle of Perseverance and Persistence

Supernatural prosperity and provision is often stopped by short-term obstacles that either come through personal failures or simply by the twists and turns of life itself. Whether or not these occurrences are short-lived or permanent is determined solely by your attitude and approach to them. Only you have the power to say how they will affect your future. What obstacle will stop you from receiving the very best of God's supernatural provision over your life? How many times have you done the following?

1. Failed to tithe on your increase.

2. |Failed to be a faithful steward of the increase God has given (i.e. let the blessing slip through your hands by spending your health or money on frivolous things).

3. Not set aside a portion of your income for a future emergency or unexpected occurrence, like the loss of a job or a medical surprise.

4. Failed to plan for the future.

5. Other personal failures.

When one of these happens, do you just give up and say that you have no control over your human nature? Or do you repent (change) and start again with a new attitude that you will continue to strive for what is right?

Persistence—or not quitting after the first personal, spiritual, moral, or financial failure—is one of the qualities that defines people of purpose.

Ephesians 6:18

With all prayer and petition pray at all times in the Spirit, and with this in view, be on the alert with all perseverance and petition for all the saints. (nasb)

Hebrews 12:1

Let us run with perseverance the race marked out for us.

2 Peter 1:5–6

For this very reason, make every effort to add to your faith goodness; and to goodness, knowledge; and to knowledge, self-control; and to self-control, perseverance; and to perseverance, godliness.

James 1:4

Perseverance must finish its work so that you may be mature and complete, not lacking anything.

Revelation 2:19

"I know your deeds, your love and faith, your service and perseverance, and that you are now doing more than you did at first."

You have probably heard how Abraham Lincoln lost every election but one prior to his being elected president of the United States. You may have also read how Thomas Edison failed more than ten thousand times prior to inventing the incandescent light. Edison's view of failure can shed interesting light on the word *persistence*. Rather than failing, he believed that he succeeded in finding ten thousand ways *not* to invent the incandescent light. In other words, the process of elimination is a vital part of the invention process.

Edison went on to say that he knew he would soon succeed because he ran out of ways that didn't work. Where would we be today if it weren't for Edison's great persistence? More recent history also points to great examples of persistence. Colonel Sanders was rejected more than a thousand times before his first successful sale of the Kentucky Fried Chicken formula. Lee Iacocca was fired from the presidency of Ford Motor Company, but his persistence led him on to even greater heights as the chairman of Chrysler Corporation. Thomas Watson, the founder of IBM, when asked about how others could emulate his great success formula, replied simply to increase their rate of failure.

Don't Give Up on Yourself

In other words, trying and failing is a risk one must bear in order to be able to try and succeed. Why? Because personal failure and personal rejection are necessary precursors to your success. You can beat up on yourself and whine about how you messed up again, or you can reread Scripture on God's desire to bless you if you will align yourself with the principles of God's Word.

You may be thinking about how many times you have tried to become spiritually aligned and failed in one area or another. But it's amazing how many weaknesses and inadequacies you can overcome if you are persistent.

Persistence is not inherited. It's a state of mind—an attitude. And since it is an attitude, it's something each of us can develop. The first step is knowing exactly what you want. If you have only a vague idea of where you're going, it's easy to give up at the first sign of a problem. You must have a clear personal goal, an intensive desire to reach it, and a definite plan that shows the path that must be followed.

If you are careless in what you do with current blessing, write out a plan to keep yourself in check. If tithing has been a problem for you, get in the habit of writing the check before you get paid and placing that check in the offering at the earliest opportunity.

You can change. You must also have faith in yourself. If you believe you can succeed in the areas of improvement you have set for yourself, setbacks along the way won't cause you to give up. You'll seldom reach a personal goal without stumbling along the way; faith in yourself enables you to get up and keep going even after slipping a bit.

The power to hold on when faced with difficulty or failure—the power to endure—this is the mantra of the overcomer. Persistence is the ability to face defeat again and again without giving up—to push on in the face of personal shortcomings and failure, knowing that victory can be yours. Persistence means taking pains to overcome every obstacle, and to do what's necessary to begin again and again.

Success in anything in life requires dogged perseverance. Before you can expect supernatural provision from God, you must be careful that your entire life is based upon biblical principles. Whether in the business world or your personal world, patience, persistence, and perseverance are conditional for improvement and ultimate blessing or success. When you fail, when you stumble, get up, get going, and get started again…and again. It's what athletes do, what business-people do, what husbands and wives do, and it should be what all Christians do. Let's look at some examples of what others have done when it comes to achieving success through personal self-discipline and persistence.

Some of the greatest and most successful people were persistent until life gave them a break. They continued to press on and eventually won because they refused to give up in self-defeat and pity.

Malcolm Forbes, the late editor-in-chief of *Forbes* magazine, one of the most successful business publications in the world, failed to make the staff of the school newspaper when he was an undergraduate at Princeton University.

After years of progressive hearing loss, by age forty-six German composer **Ludwig van Beethoven** had become completely deaf. He handled the violin awkwardly and preferred playing his own compositions rather than improving his technique. His teacher called him hopeless as a composer. Nevertheless, he wrote his greatest music, including five symphonies, during his later years.

After **Fred Astaire**'s first screen test, a 1933 memo from the MGM testing director said: "Can't act. Slightly bald. Can dance a little." Astaire kept that memo over the fireplace in his Beverly Hills home.

An expert said of famous football coach **Vince Lombardi**: "He possesses minimal football knowledge. Lacks motivation."

Louisa May Alcott, the author of *Little Women*, was advised by her family to find work as a servant or seamstress.

The teacher of famous opera singer **Enrico Caruso** said Caruso had no voice at all and could not sing.

Walt Disney was fired by a newspaper for lacking ideas. He also went bankrupt several times before he built Disneyland.

Eighteen publishers turned down **Richard Bach**'s ten-thousand-word story about a soaring seagull before Macmillan finally published it in 1970. By 1975, *Jonathan Livingston Seagull* had sold more than 7 million copies in the U.S. alone.

"As a child, **Winston Churchill** was totally rejected by preoccupied, disinterested parents. He wrote innumerable letters from boarding school pleading with his mother to visit him at Christmas.

The letters were largely unanswered, but one reply made it clear that he was not welcome at the family gathering. When the other students left to be with family during the holidays, young Winston remained alone at his school.

Churchill endured an incredibly unfortunate childhood! As well, he endured a series of failures at school and, later, political failure upon failure. It is astounding that this same Churchill would show greatness in his country's most desperate hour. Later on in his life he said something that gives insights into his greatness. He was sixty-six years old when he was asked to deliver the commencement address at Harrow, the boarding school he had attended as a youth. He stood up, looked over his glasses at the young graduates, and delivered his finest speech.

"Never, never, never give up! he cried out. With that, he sat down! In five short words Winston Churchill gave us the bottom line for success." Success is a matter of hanging on after others have let go. Here is a guideline for you to apply to your life for supernatural prosperity and provision:

- Plan purposefully
- Prepare prayerfully
- Proceed positively

- Pursue persistently

Dennis Waitley states, "Most people are like an oak tree in a flower pot; they never grow to their full potential." He states that people tend to remain cramped by poor self-belief and compressed by negative self-talk. They list reasons why they can't do it. Few launch into the exhilarating experience of breaking their own expectations with a "Yes I Can" attitude.

Leonard Ravenhill tells a fascinating story about a group of tourists in a European village. One of them asked an elderly villager, "Have any great people been born in this village?" The old villager paused and then replied, "No! Only babies." Successful people stretch for success…they dig deep into the possibilities of their God-given potential.

Successful people are not better than other people; they are ordinary people who have extraordinary attitudes—people who carry the "Yes I Can" attitude into everything they do. Remember Sir Winston Churchill, who said, "If you believe you can, you will. If you believe you can't, you won't. Either way, it's your choice."

You Are Never Too Old!

Everyone has heard of the man named Colonel Sanders. But few know how he became such a resounding success. At the age of sixty-five years, he found himself broke and alone. He received his first Social Security check for ninety-seven dollars and used it to begin promoting a chicken recipe everyone seemed to enjoy.

He started knocking on doors, telling restaurant owners his story: "I've got a great chicken recipe and I think if you use it, it'll increase your sales." Many closed the door on his face and his idea. They were too busy making the next meal to listen to a positive-thinking sixty-five-year-old salesman. But Colonel Sanders persisted—he believed he could and would do it. He focused on how to tell his story more effectively, how to get better results.

Finally, his "Yes I Can" attitude paid off. After 1009 refusals, he heard his first yes. He had spent two years driving across America in an old, beat-up car, sleeping in the backseat in his rumpled white suit, getting up each day, tired and discouraged.

But he continued to believe in his product and that someday somebody would listen. Two years of nos—1009 nos! That's why there is a KFC today.

In 1954, Ray Kroc was fifty-two years old and making his living selling milkshake machines in Southern California when he discovered his future. Kroc liked what he saw when he visited the hamburger stands of his good customers, the McDonald brothers. So he first bought the franchise rights from them; then seven years later, when he was fifty-nine, he bought the whole company for $14 million.

When he died in 1984, his personal stake in McDonald's was worth about $500 million. And he began the whole adventure at just about the age when some people are beginning to think about retirement. Ray A. Kroc, of McDonald's Corporation, posted this quote from President Coolidge on his wall:

Nothing in the world can take the place of persistence. Talent will not; nothing is more common than unsuccessful men with talent. Genius will not; unrewarded genius is almost a proverb. Education will not; the world is full of educated derelicts. Persistence and determination alone are omnipotent.

Success is connected with action. Successful people keep moving. They make mistakes, but they don't quit. Real courage is when you know you're licked before you begin, but you begin anyway and see it through no matter what.

Age isn't always a factor in your success or failure. Consider more famous examples:

- Actor George Burns won his first Oscar at eighty.

- Golda Meir was seventy-one when she became prime minister of Israel.

- Painter Grandma Moses didn't start painting until she was eighty years old. She completed over 1,500 paintings after that; 25 percent of those were produced when she was past one hundred.

- Michelangelo was seventy-one when he painted the Sistine Chapel.

- Physician and humanitarian Albert Schweitzer was still performing operations in his African hospital at eighty-nine.

- Charles Carlson developed the process of photocopying in 1938 but had to persevere for twenty-one years before the first Xerox copier finally was manufactured.

- Chuck Yeager, on his first flight as a passenger, threw up all over the backseat. He vowed never to go back up again—yet later became the first man to break the sound barrier.

- A woman once said to the great violinist Fritz Kreisler after a recital, "I'd give my life to play as beautifully as you!" "Madam," Kreisler replied, "I have."

Experiencing supernatural prosperity and provision is connected with action. Blessed people keep moving. They make mistakes, but they don't quit! Blessed people stretch for success...they dig deep into the possibilities of their God-given potential!

When you feel that being persistent is a difficult task, think of the bee. A red clover blossom contains less than one-eighth of a grain of sugar; seven thousand grains are required to make one pound of honey. A bee, flitting here and there, must visit 56,000 clover heads for one pound of honey, and there are about sixty flower tubes to each clover head. When a bee performs that operation 60 times

56,000—or 3,360,000 times—it secures enough sweetness for only one pound of honey.

"And Then Some!"

A prominent athlete summed up his fabulous success in three simple words: "And then some!"

"I discovered at an early age," he said, "that most of the differences between average and top athletes could be explained in three words. The top athletes did what was expected…and then some! The top athletes exercised hard work…and then some! They were disciplined…and then some! They gave their very best…and then some! They always met expectations…and then some! They reached to the heights of their human potential—and then some. It was the 'and then some' that turned mediocrity into excellence."

It's a rare person who doesn't get discouraged. Whether it happens to us or to a friend we're trying to cheer up, the answer centers around one word: perseverance. The value of courage, persistence, and perseverance has rarely been illustrated more convincingly than in the life story of this man:

- Failed in business   (age 22)
- Ran for legislature—defeated   (age 23)
- Again failed in business   (age 24)
- Elected to legislature   (age 25)
- Sweetheart died   (age 26)
- Had a nervous breakdown   (age 27)
- Defeated for Speaker   (age 29)
- Defeated for Elector   (age 31)
- Defeated for Congress   (age 34)

- Elected to Congress   (age 37)
- Defeated for Congress   (age 39)
- Defeated for Senate   (age 46)
- Defeated for Vice President   (age 47)
- Defeated for Senate   (age 49)
- Elected President   (age 51)

That's the record of Abraham Lincoln.

Richard Softley writes the following points about why persistence makes all the difference.

Dream Dreams

Happy are those who dream dreams and are ready to pay the price to see them come true.

Have Accurate Knowledge

Knowing that one's plans are sound and sensible encourages persistence. Be an expert in your dreams!

Have Integrity

No project will generate persistence over the long haul if it lacks in-tegrity. The idea must generate self-esteem and be good for everyone involved.

Expect Some Failure

Before success comes in any person's life, he or she is sure to meet with much temporary defeat and failure.

Always Get Up Again

When defeat overtakes a person, the easiest and most logical thing to do is quit. That is what the majority of people do. A Japanese proverb states, "Fall seven times, stand up eight."

Overcome Obstacles

President Franklin D. Roosevelt was struck down by polio, but he persevered. Unable to walk, he led the United States from a wheelchair. All obstacles can be overcome by persistence.

Reject Excuses

No blaming and no rationalizations. Never let a problem become an excuse to quit. No person has failed until they accept an "excuse."

Go All the Way

Researching third base adds no more to the score than striking out. You must go all the way.

Look Ahead Always

Never look back. "I'm not interested in the past. I'm only interested in the future, for that is where I expect to spend the rest of my life."

Stay Tough

Tough times never last, but tough people do. *Bob Schuller*

I do not think there is any other quality so essential to success of any kind as the quality of perseverance. It overcomes almost everything, even nature. *John D. Rockefeller*

What this power is I cannot say; all I know is that it exists and it becomes available only when a man is in that state of mind in which he knows exactly what he wants and is fully determined not to quit until he finds it. *Alexander Graham Bell*

Our greatest glory is not in never falling, but in rising every time we fall. *Confucius*

History has demonstrated that the most notable winners usually encountered heartbreaking obstacles before they triumphed. They won because they refused to become discouraged by their defeats. *B. C. Forbes*

Success...seems to be connected with action. Successful men keep moving. They make mistakes, but they don't quit. *Conrad Hilton*

Success seems to be largely a matter of hanging on after others have let go. *William Feather*

Effort only fully releases its reward after a person refuses to quit. *Napoleon Hill*

Most people give up just when they're about to achieve success. They quit on the one-yard line. They give up at the last minute of the game one foot from a winning touchdown. *H. Ross Perot*

It's the constant and determined effort that breaks down all resistance, sweeps away all obstacles. *Claude M. Bristol*

The majority of men meet with failure because of their lack of persistence in creating new plans to take the place of those which fail. *Napoleon Hill*

Few things are impossible to diligence and skill... Great works are performed not by strength, but perseverance. *Samuel Johnson*

Success is failure turned inside out, the silver tint of the clouds of doubt, and you never can tell how close you are, it may be near when it seems so far. So stick to the fight when you're hardest hit, it's when things seem worse, that you must not quit. *Unknown*

He conquers who endures. *Persius*

The rewards for those who persevere far exceed the pain that must precede the victory. *Ted Engstrom and R. Alec Mackenzie*

If you can force your heart and nerve and sinew to serve your turn long after they are gone, and so hold on when there is nothing in you except the will which says to them: "Hold on!" *Rudyard Kipling*

Principle 13

The Principle of Personal Provision

1 Kings 17:15–16

So she went away and did according to the word of Elijah; and she and he and her household ate for many days. The bin of flour was not used up, nor did the jar of oil run dry, according to the word of the Lord which He spoke by Elijah. (nkjv)

Supernatural provision happens when the natural is not enough. If we can make it happen on our own, there is no need for faith. No need for trusting God. And it follows that if we do not have faith and have no need for God, He will not step into areas we have reserved for our own self-control. The principle of supernatural provision is that He is strong when flesh cannot be.

Philippians 4:19

And my God will meet all your needs according to his glorious riches in Christ Jesus.

Notice that the Scripture does not say that the company that employs you will provide for your needs. Neither does it say the local banker or loan officer will supply your needs. Nor does it say that the welfare department of your government will supply your needs. It says that God, and no one else, will meet your needs. God is your only Source! It's not your job that provides your income. It is God who provides for your needs.

This story has been told for many generations. It is about a Christian family that was going through some tough times. They were so destitute that they didn't even have food for their next meal. The father and mother got down on their knees and cried out to God for food so their children would not go hungry. A man who was not a Christian was walking by their house and heard their prayer. Instead of feeling bad for them, he decided to play a trick on them.

He went down to the grocery store and bought a huge box of groceries, put it on their front porch, and rang the doorbell. When the Christian parents saw the groceries on the porch, they immediately began to thank God for it. Just then the unbeliever walked up and said, "Why are you thanking God? I'm the one who placed the groceries there." The Christian father replied, "Oh no, it was God who answered our prayer and provided the groceries. But I do want to thank you for being His delivery boy and bringing them to us!"

God is your sole source, your only provider. Through Him and Him alone are all your needs met. Your professional employment is just that. When the economy tanks, so do jobs. When the industry sector that employs you goes bust, your job disappears with it. Don't trust your education, don't trust your experience, don't trust your job—trust God.

In the natural economy, we experience such things as debt, bankruptcy, recession, depression, and other financial crises. But in God's economy there is no such thing as want, lack, recession, or depression. Yet because most of us are not aware of God's economy and His willingness to provide financial abundance, we need to be strengthened in our faith when it comes to the area of finances.

God reveals His economy by taking a "little" and turning it into "much." The most obvious example is the miracle of the feeding of the five thousand in Matthew 14. This is where Jesus took the little boy's lunch of five loaves and two fishes, blessed it, broke it, and distributed it to His disciples, who fed five thousand men, plus women and children.

Many of us, as a matter a fact, find it hard to believe that God is interested in such practical things as finances. Yet Bible scholars tell us that one out of four of the teachings of Jesus is related to our material possessions.

Another example is found in 2 Kings 4. This is a story from the life of Elisha the prophet, who gave instructions to a widow who had a need. Her late husband's creditors were about to take her two sons as slaves. She sought help from Elisha, who instructed her to collect empty jars from her neighbors and then go home and pour oil into the jars from the one jar of oil she had.

She left him and shut the door behind her and her sons. They brought the jars to her and she kept pouring. When all the jars were full, she said to her son, "Bring me another one." But he replied, "There is not a jar left." Then the oil stopped flowing. She went and told Elisha, the man of God, and he said, "Go, and sell the oil and pay your debts. You and your sons can live on what is left" (2 Kings 4:5–7).

Besides the fact that God took a little and turned it into much, we should also note that the size of the widow's blessing was dependent upon her expectancy. In other words, how much oil she received depended on how many jars she collected—the more jars, the more oil. When she got to the last jar, she probably wished she had done a better job of collecting the jars.

Principle 14

The Principle of Supernatural Provision

Supernatural provision happens when the natural is not enough. If we could make it happen on our own, there would be no need for faith. No need for trusting God. And it follows that if we do not have faith and have no need for God, He will not step into areas that we have reserved for our own self-control. The principle of supernatural provision is that He is strong when flesh cannot be. If we can make it happen on our own, there is no need for faith.

1 Kings 17:14–16

So she went away and did according to the word of Elijah; and she and he and her household ate for many days. The bin of flour was not used up, nor did the jar of oil run dry, according to the word of the Lord which He spoke by Elijah.

Genesis 24:35

The Lord has blessed my master greatly, and he has become great; and He has given him flocks and herds, silver and gold, male and female servants, and camels and donkeys. (nkjv)

Numbers 14:8

If the Lord delights in us, then He will bring us into this land and give it to us, "a land which flows with milk and honey." (nkjv)

Deuteronomy 33:23

And of Naphtali he said: "O Naphtali, satisfied with favor, and full of the blessing of the Lord, possess the west and the south." (nkjv)

Psalm 23:5

You prepare a table before me in the presence of my enemies; you anoint my head with oil; my cup runs over. (nkjv)

Psalm 36:7–8

How precious is Your loving kindness, O God! Therefore the children of men put their trust under the shadow of Your wings. They are abundantly satisfied with the fullness of Your house, and You give them drink from the river of Your pleasures. (nkjv)

Psalm 66:12

You have caused men to ride over our heads; we went through fire and through water; but You brought us out to rich fulfillment. (nkjv)

Psalm 78:15

He split the rocks in the wilderness, and gave them drink in abundance like the depths. (nkjv)

Psalm 132:15

I will abundantly bless her provision; I will satisfy her poor with bread. (nkjv)

Psalm 145:7

They shall utter the memory of Your great goodness, and shall sing of Your righteousness. (nkjv)

Psalm 147:6

The Lord lifts up the humble; He casts the wicked down to the ground. (nkjv)

Jeremiah 31:12–14

Therefore they shall come and sing in the height of Zion, streaming to the goodness of the Lord—for wheat and new wine and oil, for the young of the flock and the herd; their souls shall be like a well-watered garden, and they shall sorrow no more at all. "Then shall the virgin rejoice in the dance, and the young men and the old, together; for I will turn their mourning to joy, will comfort them, and make them rejoice rather than sorrow. I will satiate the soul of the priests with abundance, and My people shall be satisfied with My goodness, says the Lord." (nkjv)

Jeremiah 33:6–9

Behold, I will bring it health and healing; I will heal them and reveal to them the abundance of peace and truth. And I will cause the captives of Judah and the captives of Israel to return, and will rebuild those places as at the first. I will cleanse them from all their iniquity by which they have sinned against Me, and I will pardon all their iniquities by which they have sinned and by which they have transgressed against Me. Then it shall be to Me a name of joy, a praise, and an honor before all nations of the earth, who shall hear all the good that I do to them; they shall fear and tremble for all the goodness and all the prosperity that I provide for it. (nkjv)

Acts 14:17

Nevertheless He did not leave Himself without witness, in that He did good, gave us rain from heaven and fruitful seasons, filling our hearts with food and gladness. (nkjv)

Philippians 4:19

And my God shall supply all your need according to His riches in glory by Christ Jesus. (nkjv)

1 Timothy 6:17

> *Instructions to the Rich: Command those who are rich in this present age not to be haughty, nor to trust in uncertain riches but in the living God, who gives us richly all things to enjoy. (nkjv)*

Principle 15

The Principle of Supply

Philippians 4:18–20

They are a fragrant offering, an acceptable sacrifice, pleasing to God. And my God will meet all your needs according to his glorious riches in Christ Jesus.

What a great promise! We never have to be concerned about whether or not our needs will be met because we have confidence in our heavenly Father. He has assured us that because He has a more than adequate supply of riches, then we too, as His children, are entitled to those same resources. We have a secure future because of God's faithfulness. God is in control of our lives, even when we feel out of control. We can trust Him to defend us, supply our needs, guide us, and provide for us because He keeps providing for us.

Notice that the Bible does not say that God "might" supply your needs. No, He is staking His very reputation and character on the fact that He "will" supply your needs. Scripture also makes use of the simple little word all. So we are not in the queue for just one or some of our needs to be met—all of our needs will be met.

Now notice the reference to "His glorious riches." Aren't you happy that our needs being met is not dependent upon our assets, our riches, or our bank account? Scripture states that the earth is

His. His resources are much greater than ours! How about the reference to "in Christ Jesus?" If you are a born-again believer, than you are "in" Christ Jesus. The biblical promise to meet needs is not extended to everybody—just to those who have made Christ the center of their lives. But be very careful here in your expectations. He promised to supply our "needs" not our "greeds."

Principle 16

The Principle of Understanding God's Economy

Psalm 50:10

For every animal of the forest is mine, and the cattle on a thousand hills.

God's economy is different than ours. His economy is based upon a system of values and principles. Ordering your life according to His values and principles will make you successful by any measure. Living by man's values, void of all principles, will make you a loser by any measure. The values of ethics, love, compassion, giving, caring, honesty, integrity, serving, and forgiving will empower you. They have stood the test of time.

A value system built on dishonesty, lying, cheating, and stealing leads only to disaster. If your desire is to measure success by the size of check you can write, then your foundation is already shaky. God's economy measures our success by how our value system adheres to divine principles. God values whether or not we have accumulated those things that take us from this life to the next.

Much of Western culture is centered around what money can buy, and Christian culture is not immune to this! We may not be in love with money, but we are certainly enticed, maybe entrapped, by what we know money can do for us. Of course, we are part of this society, so we shouldn't think we can be completely immune to it.

Benjamin Franklin said, "Money never made a man happy yet, nor will it. There is nothing in its nature to produce happiness. The more a man has, the more he wants. Instead of filling a vacuum, it makes one."

Money and happiness are not mutually exclusive. Will Rogers said, "Too many people spend money they haven't earned to buy things they don't want, to impress people they don't like."

The Bible has a lot to say about material goods and our desire for them. The apostle Paul suggests that contentment is a very powerful value to guide us. Then he reminds us that we came into this world with nothing and will depart with nothing. He urges us to be happy when we have food and clothing and also notes that people who try to get rich quickly often fall into temptation, which often leads to disaster.

When we are successful in God's economy, we benefit both now and for eternity. If we have become successful by using this world's standards, we will always have to be on red alert, because thieves can steal, moths can destroy, and rust can corrode. If our possessions belong to God, nothing is powerful enough to take them away. So in the face of any natural economy, or even as we face death, our success will continue because we have laid up riches in heaven. Though many people possess few material goods, those who live according to the principles of God can anticipate the wealth and treasures awaiting them in heaven, which far outweigh the temporal wealth of this world.

1 Chronicles 29:10–12

Praise be to you, O Lord, God of our father Israel, from everlasting to everlasting. Yours, O Lord, is the greatness and the power and the glory and the majesty and the

*splendor, for everything in heaven and earth is yours.
Yours, O Lord, is the kingdom; you are exalted as head
over all. Wealth and honor come from you; you are
the ruler of all things. In your hands are strength and
power.*

Don't make the mistake of thinking that your job or your business is what provides your income. God is the source of your abundant supply. Jobs disappear; customers come and go. It is God who sees to it that your needs are being met. Everyone and everything else is just His instrument for getting it accomplished. God uses many vehicles to get the job done, but in the end it is not us but God's blessing upon our lives that makes it happen.

Haggai 2:8

*The silver is mine and the gold is mine, declares the
Lord Almighty.*

Billy Graham said, "If a person gets his attitude towards money straight, it will help straighten out almost every other area of his life. Tell me what you think about money, and I can tell you what you think about God, for these two are closely related. A man's heart is closer to his wallet than almost anything else."

Jesus taught that we must be responsible in our finances. God is the source of all wealth. He is the original owner of all things, for He made all things. As Scripture says, He owns the cattle on a thousand hills. In addition to the ways God provides for us supernaturally, He also gives us the ability to earn a living (Deuteronomy 8:18).

When you partner with God in business, He not only will bless it; He will let you enjoy prosperity. But there is a caution not to keep everything for yourself. When you partner with God, He will prosper you! When God becomes your source, then your well will never run dry. When we become Christians, we become children of God, and the Bible says that God wants to give gifts to His children.

Someone once said that the real measure of your wealth is how much you'd be worth if you lost all your money.

In the sixteenth century, Izaak Walton said, "Look to your health; and if you have it, praise God and value it next to conscience; for health is the second blessing that we mortals are capable of, a blessing money can't buy."

What does God already own that you are trying to keep absolute control over by refusing to acknowledge His ownership? What about your business or your house? What about your automobiles, your recreational vehicles, your clothes, your toys, and your other worldly goods?

What about your body? According to Romans 12:1, your body belongs to the Lord. Does your time belong to you or to God? What about your income, your savings, your investments, and your other possessions? Do these things belong to your or to God? Have you been allowed oversight of them for the purpose of showing good stewardship, or have you taken them over, assuming they are yours only? Everything you say, every decision you make, every action you take must be accountable to the principles of God.

What about your entire life? Your dreams, your goals, your visions—are they born of God or have you allowed your carnal nature to take complete control? Are you a thief or a steward? If a steward, then what kind of steward are you? Are you one that God can trust completely, or are you careless in your stewardship?

Not only is the silver and the gold the Lord's, so is everything else. Everything belongs to God. So why not give it all to Him? In 1 Corinthians 4:2, Paul says it is required that those who have been given a trust must prove faithful. In other words, we are all stewards and must be the kind that are faithful. A steward is simply a manager of someone else's money and possessions. We must acknowledge

God's ownership and manage it or use it as He would have us. We gain by giving; we lose by withholding.

Principle 17

The Principle of Understanding That Success Is Productivity Blessed By God

2 Corinthians 9:8–10

And God is able to provide you with every blessing in abundance, so that you may always have enough of everything and may provide in abundance for every good work. As it is written, "He scatters abroad, he gives to the poor; his righteousness endures for ever." He who supplies seed to the sower and bread for food will supply and multiply your resources and increase the harvest of your righteousness. (rsv)

Perhaps it is human nature to want something for nothing; or at least to receive a maximum amount of return for a minimum amount of effort. The old adage notes that we should work smarter, not harder. There is no doubt that the industrial revolution changed society forever. I guess that would be a good example of working smarter. But is there ever a legitimate excuse to not continue working hard?

I am from the school that says we should always work hard; we should always put forth our best effort. Does this mean that we take the most difficult path to accomplish something. Of course not. It is always important to be improving our methods of output by becoming wiser, more efficient and more productive. We do so with experience, with knowledge and with technology.

But the bottom line is this. For you to be successful with consistency, you will have to give up the ever present desire to live a life of leisure, fulfilling every personal whim and want, and choose to remain productive for a good part, if not all of your life.

God honors hard work. He honors productivity. It is my belief that God's method for success is to bless the good productive work ethics of ordinary people like you and me.

Because of our desire to maximize our benefit while minimizing our effort, we easily get into trouble. A lot of get-rich schemes prey upon unsuspecting investors. As the old proverb goes, the man who speculates is soon back to where he began—with nothing. This becomes a very serious problem, for all his or her hard work has been for nothing. It is all swept away. He or she is under a cloud; gloomy, discouraged, frustrated and angry.

Get-rich schemes without hard work, never pan out. That is simply wishful thinking. Yet, millions of dollars are lost each year to fraudulent deals because of the greed of investors.

Some people don't work to put in an honest day's work for an honest dollar, a day's work for a day's pay. They get caught up in the spirit of the fast buck. Easy money, unearned income, and a longing to get rich quick, become their pursuit!

God wants to bless you and desires for you to be successful at everything you put your hand to. But our work ethic plays a very important role in his blessing. Hard work, efficient use of our available resources, a disciplined personal life and economic opportunity will lead to prosperity and success.

You have some personal responsibilities to fulfill. Some are very basic, such as simply acknowledging that God owns it all. Others have to do with productivity, time management and learning how to plan ahead. If you are to lead a prosperous and successful life, you must apply biblical instruction to work hard and lead a disciplined live.

Then there is the responsibility of diligence, not being wasteful with our resources and knowing how to be good stewards in the handling of our possessions. We are to be accountable in caring for our assets, give generously to God and seek wisdom in matters of finances.

Biblical principles center on productivity, hard work, personal diligence and God's blessing. We are to use our God-given talents to partner with God's wisdom. If God chooses to bless us with wealth, then we properly use the riches God allows us to manage for him, to extend and further His kingdom.

I am always wary of people who openly tell others that they have an intense desire to become rich. If they are engaging their thinking during this statement, they will add the disclaimer sometime in the conversation, that their desire to become wealthy is to be able to give more to charity.

Not that there is anything wrong with riches or being wealthy, but too many people seek after it insincerely. They resist education, hard work and productivity. They seek to become rich via an inheritance or the lottery. God's way to blessing is by becoming a productive person right now regardless of your current working situation. Your roadmap to living a blessed life is through forward thinking, deliberate planning, creativity, good character, honest work, personal ingenuity and personal productivity.

Personal success is always the result of a lot of planning, intense work, good habits, and continual follow through. We are what we repeatedly do. Excellence is not an act but a habit. In fact, the only place where you will find success before work is in the dictionary. It is a planned event and rarely happens without great personal effort.

God can bless our productivity, but cannot bless the habits of a lazy person. Success comes in cans. Failure comes in cannots. Philippians 4:13 says, "I can do all things through Christ who strengthens me" (nkjv).

A very insightful proverb, whose author is unknown, follows:

Plant a thought, harvest an act.

Plant an act, harvest a habit.

Plant a habit, harvest a character.

Plant a character, harvest a destiny.

What about your regular habits? Do they lead to the blessing of God? Can God supernaturally provide for you based on your habitual acts? Are they principled, ethical, and biblically based?

Between the "where you are today" and the "where you want to be tomorrow" often stands the habits you are bound by today. Your habits keep you running in place. In the absence of some outside influence or a personal decision to do something different, your habits will keep you doing, reacting, and being the same as you've always have.

Habits are the basis for success or failure. Although people form many habits, both good and bad, habits are the basis for the future. You can form habits subconsciously or consciously. On our road to success, if we do not consciously form good habits, we will subconsciously form bad ones. Habits are not instincts; they are acquired reactions. They don't "just happen"; they are caused. Once you have determined the original cause of a habit, it is within your power to either accept or reject it.

Every person who is successful has simply formed the habits of doing things God can bless. Success and failure, happiness and unhappiness, are largely the result of habit. It is just as easy to form the habit of succeeding as it is to surrender to the habit of failure.

We are the sum total of our habits. We first form habits; then habits form us. Bad habits are easy to form. Many form automatically by default. Good habits, on the other hand, are hard to form. They never form automatically. Your number one priority should be to form good, purpose-fulfilling, goal-reaching, God-blessing habits. The attitudes and habits we cultivate measure the harvest we reap in our lives.

Blessed people can be found everywhere. They are not extraordinary people, although many have lived extraordinary lives. All have particular qualities in common. These are not qualities you inherit, but rather must be developed through education and hard work.

It's not what happens to you that counts as much as how you react to what happens. All blessed people pattern their personal and work lives after biblical principles, are productive and efficient, and actively seek the supernatural provision of God. While God will bless us abundantly, He did say that we should not eat if we don't work—*God does not bless laziness.*

Here are some things to be aware of and to work on as you seek the prosperity and provision from God.

Accept Responsibility

Attitude – Great people share one characteristic. They take obstacles and failure and convert them into motivators.

Be Flexible To Obstacles

Be Persistent.

Break Your Habits. Ask yourself, "Is there another way to accomplish this?"

Break Down Barriers To Creativity. Find the barriers to developing and implementing new ideas and remove them. Old barriers such as, "It won't work any other way; it's against policy; people won't embrace it; it's against operating procedures" just don't fit in today's management culture.

Change As Necessary.

Compassion. To offer compassion is always one of life's rich experiences.

Concentrate On Your Priorities.

Confidentiality. Don't share information you know to be confidential or that you have been asked to keep to yourself.

Determination. Be persistent, especially when you fail.

Develop a learning process. Failure isn't failure as long as we learn from it.

Effort. The only way to get something you want is to put in the effort required to get it. There are no easy answers, no get-rich-quick schemes, just plenty of scams which will only serve to derail you from your potential success.

Embrace New Perspectives. Forget your traditional perspective and approach change from other viewpoints.

Exercise. Vigorous activity strengthens your body and helps to relieve stress. Medical experts insist that people who exercise regularly, age more slowly, remain healthier and feel better than those who do not.

Giving back to others. The most treasured aspect of being successful is that it enables you to help others achieve the same.

Honesty. Always speak and live the truth.

Mentors. Learn to ask for help and support, and find resources for getting the help you need.

Minimize Interruptions That Take Away Your Focus.

Passionate pursuit. Seek the favor of God with passion.

Patience. Whether you're eager to speak next or to reach your next goal, accept that "your turn will come." This doesn't mean settling for inaction, however. Being patient isn't the same as being complacent.

Peace. Excesses of any kind can be hazardous to your physical and mental health. One must experience peace in body, soul and spirit. Take care of your body, but do not forget to care for your soul and spirit. Your emotional and spiritual health are just as necessary as your physical health.

Persistence. This is perhaps the most essential quality needed to attain success both in your professional career and in your personal life. If you throw in the towel every time you face adversity, you'll never know how a winner feels. When the going gets rough, stay in the ring and slug it out.

Practice Creativity. Try new ideas, new solutions to problems, new ways of doing things, etc.

Punctuality. Be on time, every time, every meeting, every deadline, every part of your life.

Purity. Reject anything that lowers your personal standards or the standards of those you serve.

Responsibility. Be trustworthy and dependable.

Rest. Exhaustion and stress are a dangerous combination. Do not let yourself bear the high stress of building personal dreams while at the same time depriving your body the necessary rest and relaxation that it desperately needs. By getting "rest" during the night, you'll be your "best" during the daytime.

Review Your Progress.

Seek Help.

Self-control. Make wise decisions. Don't let emotion lead you astray or let a fear of being wrong hold you back from making decisions.

Setting goals. Blessed people turn passion into practical reality.

Think In Positives And Potential. Negative thinking inhibits growth and potential.

Thoughtfulness. Think of others before yourself.

Try Out New Ways And Ideas. Don't accept, "It won't work any other way" until you've tried alternative solutions.

View Failures As Opportunities. One of the most common aspects of success is the ability and the willingness to accept the challenges failure presents.

Vision achievement. Without a vision, without purpose, no goals can be met. A lack of goals leads to a lack of planning and inaction. Know what your purpose in this life is all about. Set a vision before you.

Fill your mind with an image of what can be and what you will accomplish. Let everything in your life revolve around your vision and you'll take on track in spite of varied circumstances. Vision gives focus. Have a vision!

Blessed People Who Enjoy Prosperity and Provision...

- Are action-oriented; they get the job done.
- Their entire life and community spirit is based on biblical principles.
- They accept 100% of the responsibility for results.
- They are courageous and risk takers.

- They are faithful tithers.
- They are functionally focused; they know where they are going and how to get it done.
- They are generous givers.
- They are highly decisive; they move things forward continuously.
- They are impeccably honest.
- They are inquisitive; they don't get lazy mentally.
- They are intensely goal-oriented.
- They are persistent and committed.
- They are spiritually aligned.
- They have a sense of urgency; they get more done, and on time.
- They have above average ambition.
- They have above average willpower.
- They have purpose and seek to fulfill it.
- They have tremendous desire; they look at the reward, not the challenge.
- They welcome evaluation and assessment.

Summary

Receiving the promises of God requires a partnership between you and your Creator. While the Bible is filled with many inspiring commitments and wonderful promises from God, you know by now that there are always conditions attached. Don't be one who expects fruit from the vine, when you have not toiled in the field. The key word here is partnership. When you do what is required of you, God will always be faithful to honor the Word.

Prosperity in Scripture

Prosper

Genesis 24:40

But he said to me, 'The LORD, before whom I walk, will send His angel with you and prosper your way; and you shall take a wife for my son from my family and from my father's house. NKJV

Genesis 24:42

And this day I came to the well and said, 'O LORD God of my master Abraham, if you will now prosper the way in which I go, NKJV

Genesis 26:13

The man began to prosper, and continued prospering until he became very prosperous; NKJV

Genesis 39:3

And his master saw that the LORD was with him and that the LORD made all he did to prosper in his hand. NKJV

Genesis 39:23

The keeper of the prison did not look into anything that was under Joseph's authority, because the LORD was with him; and whatever he did, the LORD made it prosper. NKJV

Deuteronomy 28:29

And you shall grope at noonday, as a blind man gropes in darkness; you shall not prosper in your ways; you shall be only oppressed and plundered continually, and no one shall save you. NKJV

Deuteronomy 29:9

Therefore keep the words of this covenant, and do them, that you may prosper in all that you do. NKJV

Deuteronomy 30:5

Then the LORD your God will bring you to the land which your fathers possessed, and you shall possess it. He will prosper you and multiply you more than your fathers. NKJV

Joshua 1:7

Only be strong and very courageous, that you may observe to do according to all the law which Moses My servant commanded you; do not turn from it to the right hand or to the left, that you may prosper wherever you go. NKJV

Ruth 4:11

And all the people who were at the gate, and the elders, said, "We are witnesses. The LORD make the woman who is coming to your house like Rachel and Leah, the two who built the house of Israel; and may you prosper in Ephrathah and be famous in Bethlehem. NKJV

I Kings 2:3

And keep the charge of the LORD your God: to walk in His ways, to keep His statutes, His commandments, His judgments, and His testimonies, as it is written in the Law of Moses, that you may prosper in all that you do and wherever you turn; NKJV

I Kings 22:12

And all the prophets prophesied so, saying, "Go up to Ramoth Gilead and prosper, for the LORD will deliver it into the king's hand." NKJV

I Kings 22:15

Then he came to the king; and the king said to him, "Micaiah, shall we go to war against Ramoth Gilead, or shall we refrain?" And he answered him, "Go and prosper, for the LORD will deliver it into the hand of the king!" NKJV

1 Chronicles 22:11

Now, my son, may the LORD be with you; and may you prosper, and build the house of the LORD your God, as He has said to you. NKJV

1 Chronicles 22:13

Then you will prosper, if you take care to fulfill the statutes and judgments with which the LORD charged Moses concerning Israel. Be strong and of good courage; do not fear nor be dismayed. NKJV

2 Chronicles 13:12

Now look, God Himself is with us as our head, and His priests with sounding trumpets to sound the alarm against you. O children of Israel, do not fight against the LORD God of your fathers, for you shall not prosper!" NKJV

2 Chronicles 18:11

And all the prophets prophesied so, saying, "Go up to Ramoth Gilead and prosper, for the LORD will deliver it into the king's hand." NKJV

2 Chronicles 18:14

Then he came to the king; and the king said to him, "Micaiah, shall we go to war against Ramoth Gilead, or shall I refrain?" And he said, "Go and prosper, and they shall be delivered into your hand!" NKJV

2 Chronicles 20:20

So they rose early in the morning and went out into the Wilderness of Tekoa; and as they went out, Jehoshaphat stood and said, "Hear me, O Judah and you inhabitants of Jerusalem: Believe in the LORD your God, and you shall be established; believe His prophets, and you shall prosper." NKJV

2 Chronicles 24:20

Then the Spirit of God came upon Zechariah the son of Jehoiada the priest, who stood above the people, and said to them, "Thus says God: 'Why do you transgress the commandments of the LORD, so that you cannot prosper? Because you have forsaken the LORD, He also has forsaken you.' " NKJV

2 Chronicles 26:5

He sought God in the days of Zechariah, who had understanding in the visions of God; and as long as he sought the LORD, God made him prosper. NKJV

2 Chronicles 31:21

And every work which he began in the service of the house of God in law and in commandment, seeking his God, he did with all his heart and prospered. NASB

Nehemiah 1:11

O Lord, I pray, please let Your ear be attentive to the prayer of Your servant, and to the prayer of Your servants who desire to fear Your name; and let Your servant prosper this day, I pray, and grant him mercy in the sight of this man." For I was the king's cupbearer. NKJV

Nehemiah 2:20

So I answered them, and said to them, "The God of heaven Himself will prosper us; therefore we His servants will arise and build, but you have no heritage or right or memorial in Jerusalem." NKJV

Job 8:6

If you were pure and upright, surely now He would awake for you, and prosper your rightful dwelling place. NKJV

Job 12:6

The tents of robbers prosper, and those who provoke God are secure-- in what God provides by His hand. NKJV

Psalms 1:3

He shall be like a tree planted by the rivers of water, that brings forth its fruit in its season, whose leaf also shall not wither; and whatever he does shall prosper. NKJV

Psalms 122:6

Pray for the peace of Jerusalem: "May they prosper who love you. NKJV

Proverbs 3:10

Then your barns will be filled to overflowing, and your vats will brim over with new wine.

Proverbs 28:13

He who covers his sins will not prosper, but whoever confesses and forsakes them will have mercy. NKJV

Ecclesiastes 11:6

In the morning sow your seed, and in the evening do not withhold your hand; for you do not know which will prosper, either this or that, or whether both alike will be good. NKJV

Isaiah 48:15

I, even I, have spoken; yes, I have called him, I have brought him, and his way will prosper. NKJV

Isaiah 53:10

Yet it pleased the LORD to bruise Him; he has put Him to grief. When You make His soul an offering for sin, he shall see His seed, He shall prolong His days, and the pleasure of the LORD shall prosper in His hand. NKJV

Isaiah 54:17

No weapon formed against you shall prosper, and every tongue which rises against you in judgment you shall condemn. This is the heritage of the servants of the LORD, and their righteousness is from Me," says the LORD. NKJV

Isaiah 55:11

So shall My word be that goes forth from My mouth; it shall not return to Me void, but it shall accomplish what I please, and it shall prosper in the thing for which I sent it. NKJV

Jeremiah 2:37

Indeed you will go forth from him with your hands on your head; for the LORD has rejected your trusted allies, and you will not prosper by them. NKJV

Jeremiah 5:28

They have grown fat, they are sleek; yes, they surpass the deeds of the wicked; they do not plead the cause, the cause of the fatherless; yet they prosper, and the right of the needy they do not defend. NKJV

Jeremiah 10:21

For the shepherds have become dull-hearted, and have not sought the LORD; therefore they shall not prosper, and all their flocks shall be scattered. NKJV

Jeremiah 12:1

Righteous are You, O LORD, when I plead with You; yet let me talk with You about Your judgments. Why does the way of the wicked prosper? Why are those happy who deal so treacherously? NKJV

Jeremiah 20:11

But the LORD is with me as a mighty, awesome One. Therefore my persecutors will stumble, and will not prevail. They will be greatly ashamed, for they will not prosper. Their everlasting confusion will never be forgotten. NKJV

Jeremiah 22:30

Thus says the LORD: 'Write this man down as childless, a man who shall not prosper in his days; for none of his descendants shall prosper, sitting on the throne of David, and ruling anymore in Judah.' NKJV

Jeremiah 23:5-6

Behold, the days are coming," says the LORD, "That I will raise to David a Branch of righteousness; a King shall reign and prosper, and execute judgment and righteousness in the earth. In His days Judah will be saved, and Israel will dwell safely; now this is His name by which He will be called: THE LORD OUR RIGHTEOUSNESS. NKJV

Lamentations 1:5

Her adversaries have become the master, her enemies prosper; for the LORD has afflicted her because of the multitude of her transgressions. Her children have gone into captivity before the enemy. NKJV

Ezekiel 17:15

'But he rebelled against him by sending his ambassadors to Egypt, that they might give him horses and many

people. Will he prosper? Will he who does such things escape? Can he break a covenant and still be delivered? NKJV

Daniel 8:24

His power shall be mighty, but not by his own power; he shall destroy fearfully, and shall prosper and thrive; he shall destroy the mighty, and also the holy people. NKJV

Daniel 8:25

Through his cunning he shall cause deceit to prosper under his rule; and he shall exalt himself in his heart. He shall destroy many in their prosperity. He shall even rise against the Prince of princes; but he shall be broken without human means. NKJV

Daniel 11:27

Both these kings' hearts shall be bent on evil, and they shall speak lies at the same table; but it shall not prosper, for the end will still be at the appointed time. NKJV

Daniel 11:36

Then the king shall do according to his own will: he shall exalt and magnify himself above every god, shall speak blasphemies against the God of gods, and shall prosper till the wrath has been accomplished; for what has been determined shall be done. NKJV

1 Corinthians 16:2

On the first day of the week let each one of you lay something aside, storing up as he may prosper, that there be no collections when I come. NKJV

3 John 1:2

Beloved, I pray that you may prosper in all things and be in health, just as your soul prospers. NKJV

Prosperity

Deuteronomy 23:5 -6

You shall not seek their peace nor their prosperity all your days forever. NIV

Deuteronomy 28:11

And the LORD will make you abound in prosperity, in the offspring of your body and in the offspring of your beast and in the produce of your ground, in the land which the LORD swore to your fathers to give you. NASB

Deuteronomy 28:12

The LORD will open the heavens, the storehouse of his bounty, to send rain on your land in season and to bless all the work of your hands. You will lend to many nations but will borrow from none."

1 Samuel 25:5-6

And thus you shall say to him who lives in prosperity: 'Peace be to you, peace to your house, and peace to all that you have! NIV

1 Kings 10:7

However I did not believe the words until I came and saw with my own eyes; and indeed the half was not told me. Your wisdom and prosperity exceed the fame of which I heard. NIV

Ezra 9:12-13

Now therefore, do not give your daughters as wives for their sons, nor take their daughters to your sons; and never seek their peace or prosperity, that you may be strong and eat the good of the land, and leave it as an inheritance to your children forever.' NIV

Job 15:21

Dreadful sounds are in his ears; In prosperity the destroyer comes upon him. NIV

Job 21:16

Indeed their prosperity is not in their hand; the counsel of the wicked is far from me. NIV

Job 30:15

Terrors are turned upon me; They pursue my honor as the wind, and my prosperity has passed like a cloud. NIV

Job 36:11-12

If they obey and serve Him, They shall spend their days in prosperity, And their years in pleasures. But if they do not obey, They shall perish by the sword, And they shall die without knowledge. NIV

Psalms 25:13

He himself shall dwell in prosperity, And his descendants shall inherit the earth. NIV

Psalms 30:6-7

Now in my prosperity I said, "I shall never be moved." LORD, by Your favor You have made my mountain stand strong; You hid Your face, and I was troubled. NIV

Psalms 35:27

Let them shout for joy and be glad, Who favor my righteous cause; And let them say continually, "Let the LORD be magnified, Who has pleasure in the prosperity of His servant." NIV

Psalms 68:6

God sets the solitary in families; He brings out those who are bound into prosperity; But the rebellious dwell in a dry land. NIV

Psalms 73:3

For I was envious of the boastful, When I saw the prosperity of the wicked. NIV

Psalms 118:25

Save now, I pray, O LORD; O LORD, I pray, send now prosperity. NIV

Psalms 122:7

Peace be within your walls, Prosperity within your palaces." NIV

Ecclesiastes 7:14

In the day of prosperity be joyful, But in the day of adversity consider: Surely God has appointed the one as well as the other, So that man can find out nothing that will come after him. NIV

Jeremiah 22:21

I spoke to you in your prosperity, But you said, 'I will not hear.' This has been your manner from your youth, That you did not obey My voice. NIV

Jeremiah 33:9

Then it shall be to Me a name of joy, a praise, and an honor before all nations of the earth, who shall hear all the good that I do to them; they shall fear and tremble for all the goodness and all the prosperity that I provide for it.' NIV

Lamentations 3:17-18

You have moved my soul far from peace; I have forgotten prosperity. And I said, "My strength and my hope Have perished from the LORD." NIV

Daniel 4:27

Therefore, O king, let my advice be acceptable to you; break off your sins by being righteous, and your iniquities by showing mercy to the poor. Perhaps there may be a lengthening of your prosperity." NIV

Daniel 8:25

Through his cunning He shall cause deceit to prosper under his rule; And he shall exalt himself in his heart. He shall destroy many in their prosperity. He shall even rise against the Prince of princes; But he shall be broken without human means. NIV

Zechariah 1:17

Again proclaim, saying, 'Thus says the LORD of hosts: "My cities shall again spread out through prosperity; The LORD will again comfort Zion, And will again choose Jerusalem.' NIV

Acts 19:25

He called them together with the workers of similar occupation, and said: "Men, you know that we have our prosperity by this trade. NIV

Acts 24:2-4

And when he was called upon, Tertullus began his accusation, saying: "Seeing that through you we enjoy great peace, and prosperity is being brought to this nation by your foresight, we accept it always and in all places, most noble Felix, with all thankfulness. NIV

Luke 15:13

And not many days later, the younger son gathered everything together and went on a journey into a distant country, and there he squandered his estate with loose living. NASB

John 6:12

And when they were filled, He said to His disciples, "Gather up the leftover fragments that nothing may be lost." NASB

Prosperous

Genesis 24:2

And the man, wondering at her, remained silent so as to know whether the LORD had made his journey prosperous or not. NKJV

Genesis 26:13

The man began to prosper, and continued prospering until he became very prosperous; NKJV

Genesis 30:4

Thus the man became exceedingly prosperous, and had large flocks, female and male servants, and camels and donkeys. NKJV

Joshua 1:8

This Book of the Law shall not depart from your mouth, but you shall meditate in it day and night, that you may observe to do according to all that is written in it. For then you will make your way prosperous, and then you will have good success. NKJV

Judges 18:5

So they said to him, "Please inquire of God, that we may know whether the journey on which we go will be prosperous." NKJV

Psalms 22:29

All the prosperous of the earth shall eat and worship; all those who go down to the dust shall bow before Him, even he who cannot keep himself alive. NKJV

Zechariah7:7

Should you not have obeyed the words which the LORD proclaimed through the former prophets when Jerusalem and the cities around it were inhabited and prosperous, and the South and the Lowland were inhabited? NKJV

Zechariah 8:12

For the seed shall be prosperous, The vine shall give its fruit, The ground shall give her increase, and the heavens shall give their dew-- I will cause the remnant of this people To possess all these. NKJV

Success in Scripture

King James Version

Joshua 1:8

This book of the law shall not depart out of thy mouth; but thou shalt meditate therein day and night, that thou mayest observe to do according to all that is written therein: for then thou shalt make thy way prosperous, and then thou shalt have good success . KJV

American Standard Version

Joshua1:7-8

Only be strong and very courageous, to observe to do according to all the law, which Moses my servant commanded thee: turn not from it to the right hand or to the left, that thou mayest have good success whithersoever thou goest.

This book of the law shall not depart out of thy mouth, but thou shalt meditate thereon day and night, that thou mayest observe to do according to all that is written therein: for then thou shalt make thy way prosperous, and then thou shalt have good success . ASV

Amplified Version

Genesis 24:12

And he said, O Lord, God of my master Abraham, I pray You, cause me to meet with good success today, and show kindness to my master Abraham. AMP

Joshua 1:8

This Book of the Law shall not depart out of your mouth, but you shall meditate on it day and night, that you may observe and do according to all that is written in it. For then you shall make your way prosperous, and then you shall deal wisely and have good success. AMP

1 Samuel 18:30

Then the Philistine princes came out to battle, and when they did so, David had more success and behaved himself more wisely than all Saul's servants, so that his name was very dear and highly esteemed. AMP

Psalms 118:25

Save now, we beseech You, O Lord; send now prosperity, O Lord, we beseech You, and give to us success! AMP

Zechariah 8:10

For before those days there was no hire for man nor any hire for beast, neither was there any peace or success to him who went out or came in because of the adversary and oppressor, for I set (let loose) all men, every one against his neighbor. AMP

2 John 11

For he who wishes him success [who encourages him, wishing him Godspeed] is a partaker in his evil doings. AMP

New American Standard Bible

Genesis 24:11-12

And he said, "O LORD, the God of my master Abraham, please grant me success today, and show lovingkindness to my master Abraham. NASB

Joshua 1:7

Only be strong and very courageous; be careful to do according to all the law which Moses My servant commanded you; do not turn from it to the right or to the left, so that you may have success wherever you go. NASB

Joshua 1:7- 8

This book of the law shall not depart from your mouth, but you shall meditate on it day and night, so that you may be careful to do according to all that is written in it; for then you will make your way prosperous, and then you will have success . NASB

Nehemiah 2:19-20

So I answered them and said to them, "The God of heaven will give us success ; therefore we His servants will arise and build, but you have no portion, right, or memorial in Jerusalem." NASB

Job 5:12

He frustrates the plotting of the shrewd, So that their hands cannot attain success. NASB

Ecclesiastes 10:9-11

If the axe is dull and he does not sharpen its edge, then he must exert more strength. Wisdom has the advantage of giving success. NASB

Daniel 6:28

So this Daniel enjoyed success in the reign of Darius and in the reign of Cyrus the Persian. NASB

New Revised Standard Version

Genesis 24:11-13

And he said, "O LORD, God of my master Abraham, please grant me success today and show steadfast love to my master Abraham. NRSV

Genesis 27:20

But Isaac said to his son, "How is it that you have found it so quickly, my son?" He answered, "Because the LORD your God granted me success. NRSV

1 Samuel 18:14-16

David had success in all his undertakings; for the LORD was with him. 15 When Saul saw that he had great success , he stood in awe of him. 16 But all Israel and Judah loved David; for it was he who marched out and came in leading them. NRSV

1 Samuel 18:30-19:1

Then the commanders of the Philistines came out to battle; and as often as they came out, David had more success than all the servants of Saul, so that his fame became very great. NRSV

Nehemiah 1:10-11

O Lord, let your ear be attentive to the prayer of your servant, and to the prayer of your servants who delight in revering your name. Give success to your servant today, and grant him mercy in the sight of this man!" NRSV

Nehemiah 2:20

Then I replied to them, "The God of heaven is the one who will give us success , and we his servants are going to start building; but you have no share or claim or historic right in Jerusalem." NRSV

Job 5:12

He frustrates the devices of the crafty, so that their hands achieve no success . NRSV

Psalms 118:25

Save us, we beseech you, O LORD! O LORD, we beseech you, give us success ! NRSV

Isaiah 48:18-19

O that you had paid attention to my commandments! Then your prosperity would have been like a river, and your success like the waves of the sea; 19 your offspring would have been like the sand, and your descendants like its grains; their name would never be cut off or destroyed from before me. NRSV

Today's English Version

Genesis 24:12

He prayed, "LORD, God of my master Abraham, give me success today and keep your promise to my master.

Genesis 24:21

The man kept watching her in silence, to see if the LORD had given him success.

Genesis 24:40

He answered, 'The LORD, whom I have always obeyed, will send his angel with you and give you success. You will get for my son a wife from my own people, from my father's family.

Genesis 24:42

"When I came to the well today, I prayed, 'LORD, God of my master Abraham, please give me success in what I am doing.

Genesis 24:56

But he said, "Don't make us stay. The LORD has made my journey a success; let me go back to my master."

1 Samuel 18:15

Saul noticed David's success and became even more afraid of him.

1 Kings 2:33

The punishment for their murders will fall on Joab and on his descendants forever. But the LORD will always give success to David's descendants who sit on his throne."

1 Kings 21:13

The two scoundrels publicly accused him of cursing God and the king, and so he was taken outside the city and stoned to death.

1 Chronicles 12:18

God's spirit took control of one of them, Amasai, who later became the commander of "The Thirty," and he called out, "David son of Jesse, we are yours! Success to you and those who help you!

God is on your side." David welcomed them and made them officers in his army.

2 Chronicles 18:12

Meanwhile, the official who had gone to get Micaiah said to him, "All the other prophets have prophesied success for the king, and you had better do the same."

Nehemiah 1:10

Lord, these are your servants, your own people. You rescued them by your great power and strength.

Nehemiah 2:20

I answered, "The God of Heaven will give us success. We are his servants, and we are going to start building. But you have no right to any property in Jerusalem, and you have no share in its traditions."

Job 10:16

If I have any success at all, you hunt me down like a lion; to hurt me you even work miracles.

Job 20:22

At the height of his success all the weight of misery will crush him.

Psalms 35:27

May those who want to see me acquitted shout for joy and say again and again, "How great is the LORD! He is pleased with the success of his servant."

Psalms 90:17

LORD our God, may your blessings be with us. Give us success in all we do!

Psalms 118:25

Save us, LORD, save us! Give us success, O LORD!

Proverbs 8:18

I have riches and honor to give, prosperity and success.

Isaiah 48:15

I am the one who spoke and called him; I led him out and gave him success.

2 Corinthians 13:7

We pray to God that you will do no wrong — not in order to show that we are a success, but so that you may do what is right, even though we may seem to be failures.

New Living Translation

Genesis 24:12

"O LORD, God of my master," he prayed. "Give me success and show kindness to my master, Abraham. Help me to accomplish the purpose of my journey.

Genesis 24:42

"So this afternoon when I came to the spring I prayed this prayer: 'O LORD, the God of my master, Abraham, if you are planning to make my mission a success, please guide me in a special way.

Genesis 39:3

Potiphar noticed this and realized that the LORD was with Joseph, giving him success in everything he did.

Joshua 2:22

The spies went up into the hill country and stayed there three days. The men who were chasing them had searched everywhere along the road, but they finally returned to the city without success.

2 Samuel 8:10

he sent his son Joram to congratulate David on his success. Hadadezer and Toi had long been enemies, and there had been many wars between them. Joram presented David with many gifts of silver, gold, and bronze.

2 Samuel 17:20

When Absalom's men arrived, they asked her, "Have you seen Ahimaaz and Jonathan?" She replied, "They were here, but they crossed the brook." Absalom's men looked for them without success and returned to Jerusalem.

2 Samuel 23:1

These are the last words of David:
"David, the son of Jesse, speaks —
David, the man to whom God gave such wonderful success,
David, the man anointed by the God of Jacob,
David, the sweet psalmist of Israel.

2 Samuel 23:5

"It is my family God has chosen! Yes, he has made an everlasting covenant with me. His agreement is eternal, final, sealed. He will constantly look after my safety and success.

1 Kings 22:13

Meanwhile, the messenger who went to get Micaiah said to him, "Look, all the prophets are promising victory for the king. Be sure that you agree with them and promise success."

1 Chronicles 12:18

Then the Spirit came upon Amasai, who later became a leader among the Thirty, and he said, "We are yours, David! We are on your side, son of Jesse. Peace and prosperity be with you, and success to all who help you, for your God is the one who helps you." So David let them join him, and he made them officers over his troops.

1 Chronicles 18:10

he sent his son Joram to congratulate David on his success. Hadadezer and Toi had long been enemies, and there had been many wars between them. Joram presented David with many gifts of gold, silver, and bronze.

1 Chronicles 22:11

"Now, my son, may the LORD be with you and give you success as you follow his instructions in building the Temple of the LORD your God.

2 Chronicles 18:12

Meanwhile, the messenger who went to get Micaiah said to him, "Look, all the prophets are promising victory for the king. Be sure that you agree with them and promise success."

2 Chronicles 26:5

Uzziah sought God during the days of Zechariah, who instructed him in the fear of God. And as long as the king sought the LORD, God gave him success.

Ezra 5:8

We wish to inform you that we went to the construction site of the Temple of the great God in the province of Judah. It is being rebuilt with specially prepared stones, and timber is being laid in its walls. The work is going forward with great energy and success.

Nehemiah 1:11

O Lord, please hear my prayer! Listen to the prayers of those of us who delight in honoring you. Please grant me success now as I go to ask the king for a great favor. Put it into his heart to be kind to me." In those days I was the king's cup-bearer.

Job 6:13

No, I am utterly helpless, without any chance of success.

Psalms 21:3

You welcomed him back with success and prosperity. You placed a crown of finest gold on his head.

Psalms 49:18

In this life they consider themselves fortunate, and the world loudly applauds their success.

Psalms 92:7

Although the wicked flourish like weeds, and evildoers blossom with success, there is only eternal destruction ahead of them.

Psalms 118:25

Please, LORD, please save us. Please, LORD, please give us success.

Proverbs 8:14

Good advice and success belong to me. Insight and strength are mine.

Proverbs 15:22

Plans go wrong for lack of advice; many counselors bring success.

Ecclesiastes 4:4

Then I observed that most people are motivated to success by their envy of their neighbors. But this, too, is meaningless, like chasing the wind.

Daniel 11:12

After the enemy army is swept away, the king of the south will be filled with pride and will have many thousands of his enemies killed. But his success will be short lived.

John 3:29

The bride will go where the bridegroom is. A bridegroom's friend rejoices with him. I am the bridegroom's friend, and I am filled with joy at his success.

2 Corinthians 3:5

It is not that we think we can do anything of lasting value by ourselves. Our only power and success come from God.

Scriptures on God's Provision and Abundance

Genesis 27:28

May God give you of heaven's dew and of earth's richness—an abundance of grain and new wine.

Genesis 41:29

Seven years of great abundance are coming throughout the land of Egypt.

Genesis 41:30–32

But seven years of famine will follow them. Then all the abundance in Egypt will be forgotten, and the famine will ravage the land. The abundance in the land will not be remembered, because the famine that follows it will be so severe.

Genesis 41:47

During the seven years of abundance the land produced plentifully.

Genesis 41:48

Joseph collected all the food produced in those seven years of abundance in Egypt and stored it in the cities. In each city he put the food grown in the fields surrounding it.

Genesis 41:53

They will summon peoples to the mountain and there offer sacrifices of righteousness; they will feast on the abundance of the seas, on the treasures hidden in the sand.

Numbers 24:7

Water will flow from their buckets; their seed will have abundant water. "Their king will be greater than Agag; their kingdom will be exalted."

Deuteronomy 6:3

Listen obediently, Israel. Do what you're told so that you'll have a good life, a life of abundance and bounty, just as God promised, in a land abounding in milk and honey. (The Message)

Deuteronomy 28:11

The Lord will grant you abundant prosperity—in the fruit of your womb, the young of your livestock and the crops of your ground—in the land he swore to your fore-fathers to give you.

Deuteronomy 32:2

Let my teaching fall like rain and my words descend like dew, like showers on new grass, like abundant rain on tender plants.

1 Chronicles 29:16

O Lord our God, as for all this abundance that we have provided for building you a temple for your Holy Name, it comes from your hand, and all of it belongs to you.

1 Chronicles 29:21

The next day they made sacrifices to the Lord and presented burnt offerings to him: a thousand bulls, a thousand rams and a thousand male lambs, together with their drink offerings, and other sacrifices in abundance for all Israel.

2 Chronicles 11:23

He acted wisely, dispersing some of his sons throughout the districts of Judah and Benjamin, and to all the fortified cities. He gave them abundant provisions and took many wives for them.

2 Chronicles 29:35

There were burnt offerings in abundance, together with the fat of the fellowship offerings and the drink offerings that accompanied the burnt offerings. So the service of the temple of the Lord was reestablished.

Nehemiah 5:18

Each day one ox, six choice sheep and some poultry were prepared for me, and every ten days an abundant supply of wine of all kinds. In spite of all this, I never demanded the food allotted to the governor, because the demands were heavy on these people.

Nehemiah 9:25

They captured fortified cities and fertile land; they took possession of houses filled with all kinds of good things, wells already dug, vineyards, olive groves and fruit trees in abundance. They ate to the full and were well-nourished; they reveled in your great goodness.

Nehemiah 9:37

Because of our sins, its abundant harvest goes to the kings you have placed over us. They rule over our bodies and our cattle as they please. We are in great distress.

Esther 1:7

Wine was served in goblets of gold, each one different from the other, and the royal wine was abundant, in keeping with the king's liberality.

Job 36:28

The clouds pour down their moisture and abundant showers fall on mankind.

Job 36:31

This is the way he governs the nations and provides food in abundance.

Psalm 36:8

They feast on the abundance of your house; you give them drink from your river of delights.

Psalm 65:11

You crown the year with your bounty, and your carts overflow with abundance.

Psalm 66:12

You let men ride over our heads; we went through fire and water, but you brought us to a place of abundance.

Psalm 68:9

You gave abundant showers, O God; you refreshed your weary inheritance.

Psalm 73:10

Therefore their people turn to them and drink up waters in abundance.

Psalm 78:15

He split the rocks in the desert and gave them water as abundant as the seas.

Psalm 132:15

I will bless her with abundant provisions; her poor will I satisfy with food.

Psalm 144:13

Our barns will be filled with every kind of provision.

Psalm 145:7

They will celebrate your abundant goodness and joyfully sing of your righteousness.

Proverbs 12:11

He who works his land will have abundant food, but he who chases fantasies lacks judgment.

Proverbs 13:23

A poor man's field may produce abundant food, but injustice sweeps it away.

Proverbs 14:4

Where there are no oxen, the manger is empty, but from the strength of an ox comes an abundant harvest.

Proverbs 20:15

Gold there is, and rubies in abundance, but lips that speak knowledge are a rare jewel.

Proverbs 28:19

He who works his land will have abundant food, but the one who chases fantasies will have his fill of poverty.

Ecclesiastes 5:12

The sleep of a laborer is sweet, whether he eats little or much, but the abundance of a rich man permits him no sleep.

Isaiah 7:22

And because of the abundance of the milk they give, he will have curds to eat. All who remain in the land will eat curds and honey.

Isaiah 23:18

Yet her profit and her earnings will be set apart for the Lord; they will not be stored up or hoarded. Her profits will go to those who live before the Lord, for abundant food and fine clothes.

Isaiah 30:23

God will provide rain for the seeds you sow. The grain that grows will be abundant. Your cattle will range far and wide. (The Message)

Isaiah 30:33

Topheth has long been prepared; it has been made ready for the king. Its fire pit has been made deep and wide, with an abundance of fire and wood; the breath of the Lord, like a stream of burning sulfur, sets it ablaze.

Isaiah 33:23

Your rigging hangs loose: The mast is not held secure, the sail is not spread. Then an abundance of spoils will be divided and even the lame will carry off plunder.

Isaiah 66:11

"For you will nurse and be satisfied at her comforting breasts; you will drink deeply and delight in her overflowing abundance."

Jeremiah 2:22

"Although you wash yourself with soda and use an abundance of soap, the stain of your guilt is still before me," declares the Sovereign Lord.

Jeremiah 31:14

"I will satisfy the priests with abundance, and my people will be filled with my bounty," declares the Lord.

Jeremiah 33:6

"Nevertheless, I will bring health and healing to it; I will heal my people and will let them enjoy abundant peace and security."

Jeremiah 33:9

"Then this city will bring me renown, joy, praise and honor before all nations on earth that hear of all the good things I do for it; and they will be in awe and will tremble at the abundant prosperity and peace I provide for it."

Jeremiah 40:12

They all came back to the land of Judah, to Gedaliah at Mizpah, from all the countries where they had been scattered. And they harvested an abundance of wine and summer fruit.

Ezekiel 17:5

He took some of the seed of your land and put it in fertile soil. He planted it like a willow by abundant water.

Ezekiel 17:8

It had been planted in good soil by abundant water so that it would produce branches, bear fruit and become a splendid vine.

Ezekiel 19:10

Your mother was like a vine in your vineyard planted by the water; it was fruitful and full of branches because of abundant water.

Ezekiel 31:5

So it towered higher than all the trees of the field; its boughs increased and its branches grew long, spreading because of abundant waters.

Ezekiel 31:7

It was majestic in beauty, with its spreading boughs, for its roots went down to abundant waters.

Ezekiel 31:9

I made it beautiful with abundant branches, the envy of all the trees of Eden in the garden of God.

Ezekiel 31:15

This is what the Sovereign Lord says: On the day it was brought down to the grave I covered the deep springs with mourning for it; I held back its streams, and its abundant waters were restrained. Because of it I clothed Lebanon with gloom, and all the trees of the field withered away.

Ezekiel 32:13

I will destroy all her cattle from beside abundant waters no longer to be stirred by the foot of man or muddied by the hoofs of cattle.

Ezekiel 32:15

When I turn Egypt back to the wild and strip her clean of all her abundant produce, when I strike dead all who live there, then they'll realize that I am God. (The Message)

Daniel 4:12

Its leaves were beautiful, its fruit abundant, and on it was food for all. Under it the beasts of the field found shelter, and the birds of the air lived in its branches; from it every creature was fed.

Daniel 4:21

With beautiful leaves and abundant fruit, providing food for all, giving shelter to the beasts of the field, and having nesting places in its branches for the birds of the air.

Joel 2:23

Be glad, O people of Zion, rejoice in the Lord your God, for he has given you the autumn rains in righteousness. He sends you abundant showers, both autumn and spring rains, as before.

Matthew 13:12

"Whoever has will be given more, and he will have an abundance. Whoever does not have, even what he has will be taken from him."

Matthew 25:29

"For everyone who has will be given more, and he will have an abundance. Whoever does not have, even what he has will be taken from him."

Luke 12:15

Then he said to them, "Watch out! Be on your guard against all kinds of greed; a man's life does not consist in the abundance of his possessions."

Luke 21:4

"For they all gave out of their abundance (their surplus); but she has contributed out of her lack and her want, putting in all that she had on which to live." (amp)

John 10:10

"The thief comes only in order to steal and kill and destroy. I came that they may have and enjoy life, and have it in abundance (to the full, till it overflows)." (amp)

John 15:5

"I am the Vine, you are the branches. When you're joined with me and I with you, the relation intimate and organic, the harvest is sure to be abundant. Separated, you can't produce a thing." (The Message)

Romans 5:17

For if, by the trespass of the one man, death reigned through that one man, how much more will those who receive God's abundant provision of grace and of the gift of righteousness reign in life through the one man, Jesus Christ.

2 Corinthians 9:8

And God is able to make all grace (every favor and earthly blessing) come to you in abundance, so that you may always and under all circumstances and whatever the need be self-sufficient [possessing enough to require no aid or support and furnished in abundance for every good work and charitable donation]. (amp)

Philippians 4:12

I know how to be abased and live humbly in straitened circumstances, and I know also how to enjoy plenty and live in abundance. I have learned in any and all circumstances the secret of facing every situation, whether well-

fed or going hungry, having a sufficiency and enough to spare or going without and being in want. (amp)

1 Peter 1:2

Who have been chosen according to the foreknowledge of God the Father, through the sanctifying work of the Spirit, for obedience to Jesus Christ and sprinkling by his blood: Grace and peace be yours in abundance.

2 Peter 1:2

Grace and peace be yours in abundance through the knowledge of God and of Jesus our Lord.

Jude 1:2

Mercy, peace and love be yours in abundance.

Scriptures on
How to Live a Blessed Life

Accounting

Daniel 6:1–3

It pleased Darius to appoint 120 satraps to rule throughout the kingdom, with three administrators over them, one of whom was Daniel. The satraps were made accountable to them so that the king might not suffer loss.

Matthew 18:23

"Therefore, the kingdom of heaven is like a king who wanted to settle accounts with his servants."

Matthew 25:14–30

"Again, it will be like a man going on a journey, who called his servants and entrusted his property to them. To one he gave five talents of money, to another two talents, and to another one talent, each according to his ability. Then he went on his journey. The man who had received the five talents went at once and put his money to work and gained five more. So also, the one with the two talents gained two more. But the man who

had received the one talent went off, dug a hole in the ground and hid his master's money.

"After a long time the master of those servants returned and settled accounts with them. The man who had received the five talents brought the other five. 'Master,' he said, 'you entrusted me with five talents. See, I have gained five more.'

"His master replied, 'Well done, good and faithful servant! You have been faithful with a few things; I will put you in charge of many things. Come and share your master's happiness!'

"The man with the two talents also came. 'Master,' he said, 'you entrusted me with two talents; see, I have gained two more.'

"His master replied, 'Well done, good and faithful servant! You have been faithful with a few things; I will put you in charge of many things. Come and share your master's happiness!'

"Then the man who had received the one talent came. 'Master,' he said, 'I knew that you are a hard man, harvesting where you have not sown and gathering where you have not scattered seed. So I was afraid and went out and hid your talent in the ground. See, here is what belongs to you.'

"His master replied, 'You wicked, lazy servant! So you knew that I harvest where I have not sown and gather where I have not scattered seed? Well then, you should have put my money on deposit with the bankers, so that when I returned I would have received it back with interest.

"'Take the talent from him and give it to the one who has the ten talents. For everyone who has will be given more, and he will have an abundance. Whoever does not have, even what he has will be taken from him. And throw that worthless servant outside, into the darkness, where there will be weeping and gnashing of teeth.'"

Romans 14:12

So then, each of us will give an account of himself to God.

Against the Unfortunate

Deuteronomy 24:14

Do not take advantage of a hired man who is poor and needy, whether he is a brother Israelite or an alien living in one of your towns.

Psalm 10:2

In his arrogance the wicked man hunts down the weak, who are caught in the schemes he devises.

Psalm 12:5

"Because of the oppression of the weak and the groaning of the needy, I will now arise," says the Lord. "I will protect them from those who malign them."

Proverbs 14:20–21, 31

The poor are shunned even by their neighbors, but the rich have many friends. He who despises his neighbor sins, but blessed is he who is kind to the needy. He who oppresses the poor shows contempt for their Maker, but whoever is kind to the needy honors God.

Proverbs 21:13

If a man shuts his ears to the cry of the poor, he too will cry out and not be answered.

Proverbs 22:16

He who oppresses the poor to increase his wealth and he who gives gifts to the rich—both come to poverty.

Proverbs 24:23

These also are sayings of the wise: To show partiality in judging is not good.

Proverbs 28:8

He who increases his wealth by exorbitant interest amasses it for another, who will be kind to the poor.

Matthew 18:23, 34

Therefore, the kingdom of heaven is like a king who wanted to settle accounts with his servants. In anger his master turned him over to the jailers to be tortured, until he should pay back all he owed.

Luke 11:42

"Woe to you Pharisees, because you give God a tenth of your mint, rue and all other kinds of garden herbs, but you neglect justice and the love of God. You should have practiced the latter without leaving the former undone."

Luke 16:19–25

"There was a rich man who was dressed in purple and fine linen and lived in luxury every day. At his gate was laid a beggar named Lazarus, covered with sores and

longing to eat what fell from the rich man's table. Even the dogs came and licked his sores.

"The time came when the beggar died and the angels carried him to Abraham's side. The rich man also died and was buried. In hell, where he was in torment, he looked up and saw Abraham far away, with Lazarus by his side. So he called to him, 'Father Abraham, have pity on me and send Lazarus to dip the tip of his finger in water and cool my tongue, because I am in agony in this fire.'

"But Abraham replied, 'Son, remember that in your lifetime you received your good things, while Lazarus received bad things, but now he is comforted here and you are in agony."

Attitudes, Viewpoints, and Actions

Psalm 112:2–3

His children will be mighty in the land; the generation of the upright will be blessed. Wealth and riches are in his house, and his righteousness endures forever.

Psalm 112:9

He has scattered abroad his gifts to the poor, his righteousness endures forever; his horn will be lifted high in honor.

Proverbs 10:4

Lazy hands make a man poor, but diligent hands bring wealth.

Proverbs 13:4, 11

The sluggard craves and gets nothing, but the desires of the diligent are fully satisfied. Dishonest money dwindles away, but he who gathers money little by little makes it grow.

Proverbs 24:10

If you falter in times of trouble, how small is your strength!

Proverbs 28:27

He who gives to the poor will lack nothing, but he who closes his eyes to them receives many curses.

Ecclesiastes 5:12

The sleep of a laborer is sweet, whether he eats little or much, but the abundance of a rich man permits him no sleep.

Malachi 3:5

"So I will come near to you for judgment. I will be quick to testify against sorcerers, adulterers and perjurers, against those who defraud laborers of their wages, who oppress the widows and the fatherless, and deprive aliens of justice, but do not fear me," says the Lord Almighty.

Luke 6:35a

But love your enemies, do good to them, and lend to them without expecting to get anything back.

Romans 12:11

Never be lacking in zeal, but keep your spiritual fervor, serving the Lord.

Ephesians 4:28

He who has been stealing must steal no longer, but must work, doing something useful with his own hands, that he may have something to share with those in need.

Blamelessness

Psalm 1:1–2

Blessed is the man who does not walk in the counsel of the wicked or stand in the way of sinners or sit in the seat of mockers. But his delight is in the law of the Lord, and on his law he meditates day and night.

Psalm 37:37

Consider the blameless, observe the upright; there is a future for the man of peace.

Psalm 112:6

Surely he will never be shaken; a righteous man will be remembered forever.

Proverbs 10:16

The wages of the righteous bring them life, but the income of the wicked brings them punishment.

Proverbs 11:4

Wealth is worthless in the day of wrath, but righteousness delivers from death.

Proverbs 12:12

The wicked desire the plunder of evil men, but the root of the righteous flourishes.

Proverbs 16:8, 11

Better a little with righteousness than much gain with injustice. Honest scales and balances are from the Lord; all the weights in the bag are of his making.

Proverbs 19:1

Better a poor man whose walk is blameless than a fool whose lips are perverse.

Proverbs 21:3

To do what is right and just is more acceptable to the Lord than sacrifice.

Proverbs 22:1

A good name is more desirable than great riches; to be esteemed is better than silver or gold.

Proverbs 28:6, 13

Better a poor man whose walk is blameless than a rich man whose ways are perverse. He who conceals his sins does not prosper, but whoever confesses and renounces them finds mercy.

Matthew 7:20

Thus, by their fruit you will recognize them.

Luke 3:12–14

Tax collectors also came to be baptized. "Teacher," they asked, "what should we do?" "Don't collect any more than you are required to," he told them. Then some soldiers asked him, "And what should we do?" He replied, "Don't extort money and don't accuse people falsely—be content with your pay."

Luke 8:15

"But the seed on good soil stands for those with a noble and good heart, who hear the word, retain it, and by persevering produce a crop."

Luke 12:57–58

"Why don't you judge for yourselves what is right? As you are going with your adversary to the magistrate, try hard to be reconciled to him on the way, or he may drag you off to the judge, and the judge turn you over to the officer, and the officer throw you into prison."

Luke 20:22–25

"Is it right for us to pay taxes to Caesar or not?" He saw through their duplicity and said to them, "Show me a denarius. Whose portrait and inscription are on it?" "Caesar's," they replied. He said to them, "Then give to Caesar what is Caesar's, and to God what is God's."

Romans 13:7

Give everyone what you owe him: If you owe taxes, pay taxes; if revenue, then revenue; if respect, then respect; if honor, then honor.

Galatians 6:9

Let us not become weary in doing good, for at the proper time we will reap a harvest if we do not give up.

Borrowing

Exodus 22:14

If a man borrows an animal from his neighbor and it is injured or dies while the owner is not present, he must make restitution.

Deuteronomy 15:1–11

At the end of every seven years you must cancel debts. This is how it is to be done: Every creditor shall cancel the loan he has made to his fellow Israelite. He shall not require payment from his fellow Israelite or brother, because the Lord's time for canceling debts has been proclaimed. You may require payment from a foreigner, but you must cancel any debt your brother owes you. However, there should be no poor among you, for in the land the Lord your God is giving you to possess as your inheritance, he will richly bless you, if only you fully obey the Lord your God and are careful to follow all these commands I am giving you today. For the Lord your God will bless you as he has promised, and you will lend to many nations but will borrow from none. You will rule over many nations but none will rule over you. If there is a poor man among your brothers in any of the towns of the land that the Lord your God is giving you, do not be hardhearted or tightfisted toward your poor brother. Rather be openhanded and freely lend him whatever he needs. Be careful not to harbor this wicked thought: "The seventh year, the year for canceling debts, is near," so that you do not show ill will toward your needy brother and give him nothing. He may then appeal to the Lord against you, and you will be found guilty of sin. Give generously to him and do so without a grudging heart; then because of this the Lord your God will bless you in all your work and in everything you put your hand to. There will always be poor people in the land. Therefore I command you to be openhanded toward your brothers and toward the poor and needy in your land.

Psalm 37:25

I was young and now I am old, yet I have never seen the righteous forsaken or their children begging bread.

Proverbs 3:27–28

Do not withhold good from those who deserve it, when it is in your power to act. Do not say to your neighbor, "Come back later; I'll give it tomorrow"—when you now have it with you.

Proverbs 22:7

The rich rule over the poor, and the borrower is servant to the lender.

Matthew 5:25–26, 40

"Settle matters quickly with your adversary who is taking you to court. Do it while you are still with him on the way, or he may hand you over to the judge, and the judge may hand you over to the officer, and you may be thrown into prison. I tell you the truth, you will not get out until you have paid the last penny. And if someone wants to sue you and take your tunic, let him have your cloak as well."

Matthew 18:23–35

"Therefore, the kingdom of heaven is like a king who wanted to settle accounts with his servants. As he began the settlement, a man who owed him ten thousand talents was brought to him. Since he was not able to pay, the master ordered that he and his wife and his children and all that he had be sold to repay the debt.

"The servant fell on his knees before him. 'Be patient with me,' he begged, 'and I will pay back everything.' The servant's master took pity on him, canceled the debt and let him go.

"But when that servant went out, he found one of his fellow servants who owed him a hundred denarii. He grabbed him and began to choke him. 'Pay back what you owe me!' he demanded.

"His fellow servant fell to his knees and begged him, 'Be patient with me, and I will pay you back.'

"But he refused. Instead, he went off and had the man thrown into prison until he could pay the debt. When the other servants saw what had happened, they were greatly distressed and went and told their master everything that had happened.

"Then the master called the servant in. 'You wicked servant,' he said, 'I canceled all that debt of yours because you begged me to. Shouldn't you have had mercy on your fellow servant just as I had on you?' In anger his master turned him over to the jailers to be tortured, until he should pay back all he owed.

"This is how my heavenly Father will treat each of you unless you forgive your brother from your heart."

Budgeting

Proverbs 16:9

In his heart a man plans his course, but the Lord determines his steps.

Proverbs 19:21

Many are the plans in a man's heart, but it is the Lord's purpose that prevails.

Proverbs 22:3

A prudent man sees danger and takes refuge, but the simple keep going and suffer for it.

Proverbs 24:3–4

By wisdom a house is built, and through understanding it is established; through knowledge its rooms are filled with rare and beautiful treasures.

Proverbs 27:12

The prudent see danger and take refuge, but the simple keep going and suffer for it.

Luke 12:16–21

And he told them this parable: "The ground of a certain rich man produced a good crop. He thought to himself, What shall I do? I have no place to store my crops.

"Then he said, 'This is what I'll do. I will tear down my barns and build bigger ones, and there I will store all my grain and my goods. And I'll say to myself, You have plenty of good things laid up for many years. Take life easy; eat, drink and be merry.

"But God said to him, 'You fool! This very night your life will be demanded from you. Then who will get what you have prepared for yourself?'

"This is how it will be with anyone who stores up things for himself but is not rich toward God."

Luke 14:28–30

"Suppose one of you wants to build a tower. Will he not first sit down and estimate the cost to see if he has enough money to complete it? For if he lays the foundation and is not able to finish it, everyone who sees it will ridicule him, saying, 'This fellow began to build and was not able to finish.'"

Luke 16:1–8

Jesus told his disciples: "There was a rich man whose manager was accused of wasting his possessions. So he called him in and asked him, 'What is this I hear about you? Give an account of your management, because you cannot be manager any longer.'

"The manager said to himself, 'What shall I do now? My master is taking away my job. I'm not strong enough to dig, and I'm ashamed to beg—I know what I'll do so that, when I lose my job here, people will welcome me into their houses.'

"So he called in each one of his master's debtors. He asked the first, 'How much do you owe my master?'

"'Eight hundred gallons of olive oil,' he replied.

"The manager told him, 'Take your bill, sit down quickly, and make it four hundred.'

"Then he asked the second, 'And how much do you owe?'

"'A thousand bushels of wheat,' he replied.

"He told him, 'Take your bill and make it eight hundred.'

"The master commended the dishonest manager because he had acted shrewdly. For the people of this world are more shrewd in dealing with their own kind than are the people of the light."

1 Corinthians 16:1–2

Now about the collection for God's people: Do what I told the Galatian churches to do. On the first day of every week, each one of you should set aside a sum of money in keeping with his income, saving it up, so that when I come no collections will have to be made.

Caution

Proverbs 8:12

I, wisdom, dwell together with prudence; I possess knowledge and discretion.

Proverbs 12:16, 23

A fool shows his annoyance at once, but a prudent man overlooks an insult. A prudent man keeps his knowledge to himself, but the heart of fools blurts out folly.

Proverbs 13:16

Every prudent man acts out of knowledge, but a fool exposes his folly.

Proverbs 14:8, 15, 18

The wisdom of the prudent is to give thought to their ways, but the folly of fools is deception. A simple man believes anything, but a prudent man gives thought to his steps. The simple inherit folly, but the prudent are crowned with knowledge.

Proverbs 15:5

A fool spurns his father's discipline, but whoever heeds correction shows prudence.

Proverbs 16:21

The wise in heart are called discerning, and pleasant words promote instruction.

Proverbs 18:15

The heart of the discerning acquires knowledge; the ears of the wise seek it out.

Proverbs 22:3

A prudent man sees danger and takes refuge, but the simple keep going and suffer for it.

Proverbs 27:12

The prudent see danger and take refuge, but the simple keep going and suffer for it.

Hosea 14:9

Who is wise? He will realize these things. Who is discerning? He will understand them. The ways of the Lord are right; the righteous walk in them, but the rebellious stumble in them.

Amos 5:13

This is what the Sovereign Lord says: "The city that marches out a thousand strong for Israel will have only a hundred left; the town that marches out a hundred strong will have only ten left."

Contentment

Joshua 7:7

And Joshua said, "Ah, Sovereign Lord, why did you ever bring this people across the Jordan to deliver us into the hands of the Amorites to destroy us? If only we had been content to stay on the other side of the Jordan!"

Proverbs 30:7–9

"Two things I ask of you, O Lord; do not refuse me before I die: Keep falsehood and lies far from me; give me neither poverty nor riches, but give me only my daily bread. Otherwise, I may have too much and disown you and say, 'Who is the Lord?' Or I may become poor and steal, and so dishonor the name of my God."

Matthew 20:1–16

"For the kingdom of heaven is like a landowner who went out early in the morning to hire men to work in his vineyard. He agreed to pay them a denarius for the day and sent them into his vineyard.

"About the third hour he went out and saw others standing in the marketplace doing nothing. He told them, 'You also go and work in my vineyard, and I will pay you whatever is right.' So they went.

"He went out again about the sixth hour and the ninth hour and did the same thing. About the eleventh hour he went out and found still others standing around. He asked them, 'Why have you been standing here all day long doing nothing?'

"'Because no one has hired us,' they answered. "He said to them, 'You also go and work in my vineyard.'

"When evening came, the owner of the vineyard said to his foreman, 'Call the workers and pay them their wages, beginning with the last ones hired and going on to the first.'

"The workers who were hired about the eleventh hour came and each received a denarius. So when those came who were hired first, they expected to receive more. But each one of them also received a denarius. When they received it, they began to grumble against the landowner. 'These men who were hired last worked only one hour,' they said, 'and you have made them equal to us who have borne the burden of the work and the heat of the day.'

"But he answered one of them, 'Friend, I am not being unfair to you. Didn't you agree to work for a denarius? Take your pay and go. I want to give the man who was hired last the same as I gave you. Don't I have the right to do what I want with my own money? Or are you envious because I am generous?'

"So the last will be first, and the first will be last."

2 Corinthians 6:10

Sorrowful, yet always rejoicing; poor, yet making many rich; having nothing, and yet possessing everything.

Philippians 4:11–12

I am not saying this because I am in need, for I have learned to be content whatever the circumstances. I know what it is to be in need, and I know what it is to have plenty. I have learned the secret of being content in any and every situation, whether well fed or hungry, whether living in plenty or in want.

Colossians 3:2

Set your minds on things above, not on earthly things.

1 Thessalonians 5:16–18

Be joyful always; pray continually; give thanks in all circumstances, for this is God's will for you in Christ Jesus.

1 Timothy 6:6–10

But godliness with contentment is great gain. For we brought nothing into the world, and we can take noth-

ing out of it. But if we have food and clothing, we will be content with that. People who want to get rich fall into temptation and a trap and into many foolish and harmful desires that plunge men into ruin and destruction. For the love of money is a root of all kinds of evil. Some people, eager for money, have wandered from the faith and pierced themselves with many griefs.

Hebrews 13:5

Keep your lives free from the love of money and be content with what you have, because God has said, "Never will I leave you; never will I forsake you."

Counsel

Proverbs 3:13

Blessed is the man who finds wisdom, the man who gains understanding,

Proverbs 12:5, 15

The plans of the righteous are just, but the advice of the wicked is deceitful. The way of a fool seems right to him, but a wise man listens to advice.

Proverbs 13:20

He who walks with the wise grows wise, but a companion of fools suffers harm.

Proverbs 14:7

Stay away from a foolish man, for you will not find knowledge on his lips.

Proverbs 15:22

Plans fail for lack of counsel, but with many advisers they succeed.

Proverbs 19:20

Listen to advice and accept instruction, and in the end you will be wise.

Proverbs 24:3, 6

By wisdom a house is built, and through understanding it is established; for waging war you need guidance, and for victory many advisers.

Proverbs 27:9

Perfume and incense bring joy to the heart, and the pleasantness of one's friend springs from his earnest counsel.

Cosigning Notes

Proverbs 6:1–5

My son, if you have put up security for your neighbor, if you have struck hands in pledge for another, if you have been trapped by what you said, ensnared by the words of your mouth, then do this, my son, to free yourself, since you have fallen into your neighbor's hands: Go and humble yourself; press your plea with your neighbor! Allow no sleep to your eyes, no slumber to your eyelids. Free yourself, like a gazelle from the hand of the hunter, like a bird from the snare of the fowler.

Proverbs 11:15

He who puts up security for another will surely suffer, but whoever refuses to strike hands in pledge is safe.

Proverbs 17:18

A man lacking in judgment strikes hands in pledge and puts up security for his neighbor.

Proverbs 20:16

Take the garment of one who puts up security for a stranger; hold it in pledge if he does it for a wayward woman.

Proverbs 22:26

Do not be a man who strikes hands in pledge or puts up security for debts.

Proverbs 27:13

Take the garment of one who puts up security for a stranger; hold it in pledge if he does it for a wayward woman.

Debt

Deuteronomy 15:6

For the Lord your God will bless you as he has promised, and you will lend to many nations but will borrow from none. You will rule over many nations but none will rule over you.

Deuteronomy 28:12–13

The Lord will open the heavens, the storehouse of his bounty, to send rain on your land in season and to bless all the work of your hands. You will lend to many nations but will borrow from none. The Lord will make you the head, not the tail. If you pay attention to the commands of the Lord your God that I give you this day and carefully follow them, you will always be at the top, never at the bottom.

2 Kings 4:1–7

The wife of a man from the company of the prophets cried out to Elisha, "Your servant my husband is dead, and you know that he revered the Lord. But now his creditor is coming to take my two boys as his slaves." Elisha replied to her, "How can I help you? Tell me, what do you have in your house?" "Your servant has nothing there at all," she said, "except a little oil." Elisha said, "Go around and ask all your neighbors for empty jars. Don't ask for just a few. Then go inside and shut the door behind you and your sons. Pour oil into all the jars, and as each is filled, put it to one side." She left him and afterward shut the door behind her and her sons. They brought the jars to her and she kept pouring. When all the jars were full, she said to her son, "Bring me another one." But he replied, "There is not a jar left." Then the oil stopped flowing. She went and told the man of God, and he said, "Go, sell the oil and pay your debts. You and your sons can live on what is left."

Psalm 37:21

The wicked borrow and do not repay, but the righteous give generously;

Proverbs 3:27–28

Do not withhold good from those who deserve it, when it is in your power to act. Do not say to your neighbor, "Come back later; I'll give it tomorrow"—when you now have it with you.

Proverbs 6:1–3

My son, if you have put up security for your neighbor, if you have struck hands in pledge for another, if you have been trapped by what you said, ensnared by the words of your mouth, then do this, my son, to free yourself, since you have fallen into your neighbor's hands: Go and humble yourself; press your plea with your neighbor!

Proverbs 11:15

He who puts up security for another will surely suffer, but whoever refuses to strike hands in pledge is safe.

Proverbs 17:18

A man lacking in judgment strikes hands in pledge and puts up security for his neighbor.

Proverbs 22:7

The rich rule over the poor, and the borrower is servant to the lender.

Proverbs 27:13

Take the garment of one who puts up security for a stranger; hold it in pledge if he does it for a wayward woman.

Matthew 5:25–26

"Settle matters quickly with your adversary who is taking you to court. Do it while you are still with him on

the way, or he may hand you over to the judge, and the judge may hand you over to the officer, and you may be thrown into prison. I tell you the truth, you will not get out until you have paid the last penny."

Matthew 18:23

"Therefore, the kingdom of heaven is like a king who wanted to settle accounts with his servants."

Romans 13:8

Let no debt remain outstanding, except the continuing debt to love one another, for he who loves his fellowman has fulfilled the law.

Diligence

Proverbs 6:4

Allow no sleep to your eyes, no slumber to your eyelids.

Proverbs 12:11, 24

He who works his land will have abundant food, but he who chases fantasies lacks judgment. Diligent hands will rule, but laziness ends in slave labor.

Proverbs 13:11

Dishonest money dwindles away, but he who gathers money little by little makes it grow.

Proverbs 14:4

Where there are no oxen, the manger is empty, but from the strength of an ox comes an abundant harvest.

Proverbs 16:3

Commit to the Lord whatever you do, and your plans will succeed.

Proverbs 21:5

The plans of the diligent lead to profit as surely as haste leads to poverty.

Proverbs 24:3–4, 7

By wisdom a house is built, and through understanding it is established; through knowledge its rooms are filled with rare and beautiful treasures. Wisdom is too high for a fool; in the assembly at the gate he has nothing to say.

Matthew 20:13

"But he answered one of them, 'Friend, I am not being unfair to you. Didn't you agree to work for a denarius?'"

2 Timothy 2:6

The hardworking farmer should be the first to receive a share of the crops.

1 Thessalonians 4:11

Make it your ambition to lead a quiet life, to mind your own business and to work with your hands, just as we told you.

Dishonesty

Psalm 37:37

Consider the blameless, observe the upright; there is a future for the man of peace.

Psalm 15:5

Who lends his money without usury and does not accept a bribe against the innocent. He who does these things will never be shaken.

Psalm 62:10–12

Do not trust in extortion or take pride in stolen goods; though your riches increase, do not set your heart on them. One thing God has spoken, two things have I heard: that you, O God, are strong, and that you, O Lord, are loving. Surely you will reward each person according to what he has done.

Proverbs 10:15–16

The wealth of the rich is their fortified city, but poverty is the ruin of the poor. The wages of the righteous bring them life, but the income of the wicked brings them punishment.

Proverbs 11:1, 16, 18

The Lord abhors dishonest scales, but accurate weights are his delight. A kindhearted woman gains respect, but ruthless men gain only wealth. The wicked man earns deceptive wages, but he who sows righteousness reaps a sure reward.

Proverbs 12:3, 12

A man cannot be established through wickedness, but the righteous cannot be uprooted. The wicked desire the plunder of evil men, but the root of the righteous flourishes.

Proverbs 13:7, 11

One man pretends to be rich, yet has nothing; another pretends to be poor, yet has great wealth. Dishonest money dwindles away, but he who gathers money little by little makes it grow.

Proverbs 15:6, 27

The house of the righteous contains great treasure, but the income of the wicked brings them trouble. A greedy man brings trouble to his family, but he who hates bribes will live.

Proverbs 16:2, 11

All a man's ways seem innocent to him, but motives are weighed by the Lord. Honest scales and balances are from the Lord; all the weights in the bag are of his making.

Proverbs 17:2

A wise servant will rule over a disgraceful son, and will share the inheritance as one of the brothers.

Proverbs 20:21

An inheritance quickly gained at the beginning will not be blessed at the end.

Proverbs 22:28

Do not move an ancient boundary stone set up by your forefathers.

Proverbs 24:16, 19–20

For though a righteous man falls seven times, he rises again, but the wicked are brought down by calamity. Do not fret because of evil men or be envious of the wicked, for the evil man has no future hope, and the lamp of the wicked will be snuffed out.

Proverbs 28:6, 18

Better a poor man whose walk is blameless than a rich man whose ways are perverse. He whose walk is blameless is kept safe, but he whose ways are perverse will suddenly fall.

Jeremiah 9:4

Beware of your friends; do not trust your brothers. For every brother is a deceiver, and every friend a slanderer.

Matthew 18:7

Woe to the world because of the things that cause people to sin! Such things must come, but woe to the man through whom they come!

Matthew 27:5

So Judas threw the money into the temple and left. Then he went away and hanged himself.

Luke 9:25

What good is it for a man to gain the whole world, and yet lose or forfeit his very self?

Luke 11:42

Woe to you Pharisees, because you give God a tenth of your mint, rue and all other kinds of garden herbs, but you neglect justice and the love of God. You should have practiced the latter without leaving the former undone.

Luke 16:1, 10–14

Jesus told his disciples: "There was a rich man whose manager was accused of wasting his possessions.

"Whoever can be trusted with very little can also be trusted with much, and whoever is dishonest with very little will also be dishonest with much. So if you have not been trustworthy in handling worldly wealth, who will trust you with true riches? And if you have not been trustworthy with someone else's property, who will give you property of your own?

"No servant can serve two masters. Either he will hate the one and love the other, or he will be devoted to the one and despise the other. You cannot serve both God and Money."

The Pharisees, who loved money, heard all this and were sneering at Jesus.

Luke 19:8

But Zacchaeus stood up and said to the Lord, "Look, Lord! Here and now I give half of my possessions to the poor, and if I have cheated anybody out of anything, I will pay back four times the amount."

Luke 20:46–47

"Beware of the teachers of the law. They like to walk around in flowing robes and love to be greeted in the marketplaces and have the most important seats in the synagogues and the places of honor at banquets. They devour widows' houses and for a show make lengthy prayers. Such men will be punished most severely."

Romans 2:21–22

You, then, who teach others, do you not teach yourself? You who preach against stealing, do you steal? You who say that people should not commit adultery, do you commit adultery? You who abhor idols, do you rob temples?

Ego

Psalm 75:4

To the arrogant I say, "Boast no more," and to the wicked, "Do not lift up your horns."

Psalm 107:40

He who pours contempt on nobles made them wander in a trackless waste.

Proverbs 11:2

When pride comes, then comes disgrace, but with humility comes wisdom.

Proverbs 12:9

Better to be a nobody and yet have a servant than pretend to be somebody and have no food.

Proverbs 15:25

The Lord tears down the proud man's house but he keeps the widow's boundaries intact.

Proverbs 16:18–19

Pride goes before destruction, a haughty spirit before a fall. Better to be lowly in spirit and among the oppressed than to share plunder with the proud.

Proverbs 18:12, 23

Before his downfall a man's heart is proud, but humility comes before honor. A poor man pleads for mercy, but a rich man answers harshly.

Proverbs 19:1

Better a poor man whose walk is blameless than a fool whose lips are perverse.

Proverbs 28:11

A rich man may be wise in his own eyes, but a poor man who has discernment sees through him.

Proverbs 29:23

A man's pride brings him low, but a man of lowly spirit gains honor.

Jeremiah 9:23

This is what the Lord says: "Let not the wise man boast of his wisdom or the strong man boast of his strength or the rich man boast of his riches."

Jeremiah 22:21

I warned you when you felt secure, but you said, "I will not listen!" This has been your way from your youth; you have not obeyed me.

Matthew 23:12

"For whoever exalts himself will be humbled, and whoever humbles himself will be exalted."

Luke 14:11

"For everyone who exalts himself will be humbled, and he who humbles himself will be exalted."

Philippians 2:3

Do nothing out of selfish ambition or vain conceit, but in humility consider others better than yourselves.

1 Timothy 6:17

Command those who are rich in this present world not to be arrogant nor to put their hope in wealth, which is so uncertain, but to put their hope in God, who richly provides us with everything for our enjoyment.

Envy

Psalm 73:2

But as for me, my feet had almost slipped; I had nearly lost my foothold.

Proverbs 23:17

Do not let your heart envy sinners, but always be zealous for the fear of the Lord.

Proverbs 24:19

Do not fret because of evil men or be envious of the wicked,

Excellence

Proverbs 18:9

One who is slack in his work is brother to one who destroys.

Proverbs 22:29

Do you see a man skilled in his work? He will serve before kings; he will not serve before obscure men.

Colossians 3:17, 23

And whatever you do, whether in word or deed, do it all in the name of the Lord Jesus, giving thanks to God the Father through him. Whatever you do, work at it with all your heart, as working for the Lord, not for men,

1 Peter 4:11

If anyone speaks, he should do it as one speaking the very words of God. If anyone serves, he should do it with the strength God provides, so that in all things God may be praised through Jesus Christ. To him be the glory and the power for ever and ever. Amen.

Getting the Facts

Proverbs 14:8, 15

The wisdom of the prudent is to give thought to their ways, but the folly of fools is deception. A simple man believes anything, but a prudent man gives thought to his steps.

Proverbs 18:13

He who answers before listening—that is his folly and his shame.

Proverbs 19:2

It is not good to have zeal without knowledge, nor to be hasty and miss the way.

Proverbs 23:23

Buy the truth and do not sell it; get wisdom, discipline and understanding.

Proverbs 27:23–24

Be sure you know the condition of your flocks, give careful attention to your herds; for riches do not endure forever, and a crown is not secure for all generations.

James 1:5

If any of you lacks wisdom, he should ask God, who gives generously to all without finding fault, and it will be given to him.

Giving

Isaiah 66:20

And they will bring all your brothers, from all the nations, to my holy mountain in Jerusalem as an offering to the Lord—on horses, in chariots and wagons, and on mules and camels," says the Lord. "They will bring them, as the Israelites bring their grain offerings, to the temple of the Lord in ceremonially clean vessels.

Psalm 96:7–8

Ascribe to the Lord, O families of nations, ascribe to the Lord glory and strength. Ascribe to the Lord the glory due his name; bring an offering and come into his courts.

Psalm 112:5

Good will come to him who is generous and lends freely, who conducts his affairs with justice.

Proverbs 3:9–10

Honor the Lord with your wealth, with the firstfruits of all your crops; then your barns will be filled to overflowing, and your vats will brim over with new wine.

Proverbs 11:24–26

One man gives freely, yet gains even more; another withholds unduly, but comes to poverty. A generous man will prosper; he who refreshes others will himself be refreshed. People curse the man who hoards grain, but blessing crowns him who is willing to sell.

Proverbs 28:22

A stingy man is eager to get rich and is unaware that poverty awaits him.

Mark 4:24

"Consider carefully what you hear," he continued. "With the measure you use, it will be measured to you—and even more."

Mark 12:41–44

Jesus sat down opposite the place where the offerings were put and watched the crowd putting their money into the temple treasury. Many rich people threw in large amounts. But a poor widow came and put in two very small copper coins, worth only a fraction of a penny. Calling his disciples to him, Jesus said, "I tell you the truth, this poor widow has put more into the treasury than all the others. They all gave out of their wealth; but she, out of her poverty, put in everything-all she had to live on."

Luke 6:38

"Give, and it will be given to you. A good measure, pressed down, shaken together and running over, will be poured into your lap. For with the measure you use, it will be measured to you."

Acts 2:45

Selling their possessions and goods, they gave to anyone as he had need.

Greed

Psalm 73:2–3, 17, 20

But as for me, my feet had almost slipped; I had nearly lost my foothold. For I envied the arrogant when I saw the prosperity of the wicked. Till I entered the sanctuary of God; then I understood their final destiny. As a dream when one awakes, so when you arise, O Lord, you will despise them as fantasies.

Proverbs 23:4–5

Do not wear yourself out to get rich; have the wisdom to show restraint. Cast but a glance at riches, and they are gone, for they will surely sprout wings and fly off to the sky like an eagle.

Proverbs 28:25

A greedy man stirs up dissension, but he who trusts in the Lord will prosper.

Luke 12:15

Then he said to them, "Watch out! Be on your guard against all kinds of greed; a man's life does not consist in the abundance of his possessions."

Luke 18:24

Jesus looked at him and said, "How hard it is for the rich to enter the kingdom of God!"

Ephesians 5:5

For of this you can be sure: No immoral, impure or greedy person—such a man is an idolater—has any inheritance in the kingdom of Christ and of God.

Helping the Unfortunate

Psalm 69:33

The Lord hears the needy and does not despise his captive people.

Psalm 72:1, 4–15, 17

Endow the king with your justice, O God, the royal son with your righteousness. He will defend the afflicted among the people and save the children of the needy; he will crush the oppressor. He will endure as long as the sun, as long as the moon, through all generations. He will be like rain falling on a mown field, like showers watering the earth. In his days the righteous will flourish; prosperity will abound till the moon is no more. He will rule from sea to sea and from the River to the ends of the earth. The desert tribes will bow before him and his enemies will lick the dust. The kings of Tarshish and of distant shores will bring tribute to him; the kings of Sheba and Seba will present him gifts. All kings will bow down to him and all nations will serve him. For he will deliver the needy who cry out, the afflicted who have no one to help. He will take pity on the weak and the needy and save the needy from death. He will rescue them from oppression and violence, for precious is their blood in his sight. Long may he live! May gold from Sheba be given him. May people ever pray for him and bless him all day long. May his name endure forever; may it continue as long as the sun. All nations will be blessed through him, and they will call him blessed.

Psalm 109:31

For he stands at the right hand of the needy one, to save his life from those who condemn him.

Proverbs 14:21

He who despises his neighbor sins, but blessed is he who is kind to the needy.

Proverbs 14:31

He who oppresses the poor shows contempt for their Maker, but whoever is kind to the needy honors God.

Matthew 5:42

"Give to the one who asks you, and do not turn away from the one who wants to borrow from you."

Matthew 6:19–20

"Do not store up for yourselves treasures on earth, where moth and rust destroy, and where thieves break in and steal. But store up for yourselves treasures in heaven, where moth and rust do not destroy, and where thieves do not break in and steal."

Matthew 10:42

"And if anyone gives even a cup of cold water to one of these little ones because he is my disciple, I tell you the truth, he will certainly not lose his reward."

Luke 3:11

John answered, "The man with two tunics should share with him who has none, and the one who has food should do the same."

Luke 9:48

Then he said to them, "Whoever welcomes this little child in my name welcomes me; and whoever welcomes me welcomes the one who sent me. For he who is least among you all—he is the greatest."

Luke 10:35

"The next day he took out two silver coins and gave them to the innkeeper. 'Look after him,' he said, 'and when I return, I will reimburse you for any extra expense you may have.'"

Luke 12:33

"Sell your possessions and give to the poor. Provide purses for yourselves that will not wear out, a treasure in heaven that will not be exhausted, where no thief comes near and no moth destroys."

Luke 19:8–9

But Zacchaeus stood up and said to the Lord, "Look, Lord! Here and now I give half of my possessions to the poor, and if I have cheated anybody out of anything, I will pay back four times the amount." Jesus said to him, "Today salvation has come to this house, because this man, too, is a son of Abraham."

1 Timothy 5:3, 8, 15–16

Give proper recognition to those widows who are really in need. If anyone does not provide for his relatives, and especially for his immediate family, he has denied the faith and is worse than an unbeliever. Some have in fact already turned away to follow Satan. If any woman who is a believer has widows in her family, she should help them and not let the church be burdened with them, so that the church can help those widows who are really in need.

1 John 3:17

If anyone has material possessions and sees his brother in need but has no pity on him, how can the love of God be in him?

Hoarding

Psalm 49:11, 16–17

Their tombs will remain their houses forever, their dwellings for endless generations, though they had named lands after themselves. Do not be overawed when a man grows rich, when the splendor of his house increases; for he will take nothing with him when he dies, his splendor will not descend with him.

Proverbs 13:22

A good man leaves an inheritance for his children's children, but a sinner's wealth is stored up for the righteous.

Proverbs 28:22

A stingy man is eager to get rich and is unaware that poverty awaits him.

Malachi 1:7, 9

You place defiled food on my altar. "But you ask, 'How have we defiled you?'

"By saying that the Lord's table is contemptible.

"Now implore God to be gracious to us. With such offerings from your hands, will he accept you?" says the Lord Almighty.

Malachi 3:8

"Will a man rob God? Yet you rob me. But you ask, 'How do we rob you?' In tithes and offerings."

Matthew 6:24

"No one can serve two masters. Either he will hate the one and love the other, or he will be devoted to the one and despise the other. You cannot serve both God and Money."

Matthew 19:23

Then Jesus said to his disciples, "I tell you the truth, it is hard for a rich man to enter the kingdom of heaven."

Luke 12:21, 33

"This is how it will be with anyone who stores up things for himself but is not rich toward God. Sell your possessions and give to the poor. Provide purses for yourselves that will not wear out, a treasure in heaven that will not be exhausted, where no thief comes near and no moth destroys."

Honesty

Deuteronomy 25:14–15

Do not have two differing measures in your house—one large, one small. You must have accurate and honest weights and measures, so that you may live long in the land the Lord your God is giving you.

Psalm 112:1–3, 5

Praise the Lord. Blessed is the man who fears the Lord, who finds great delight in his commands. His children will be mighty in the land; the generation of the upright will be blessed. Wealth and riches are in his house, and his righteousness endures forever. Good will come to him who is generous and lends freely, who conducts his affairs with justice.

Proverbs 10:3, 9

The Lord does not let the righteous go hungry but he thwarts the craving of the wicked. The man of integrity walks securely, but he who takes crooked paths will be found out.

Proverbs 13:5, 11, 21

The righteous hate what is false, but the wicked bring shame and disgrace. Dishonest money dwindles away, but he who gathers money little by little makes it grow. Misfortune pursues the sinner, but prosperity is the reward of the righteous.

Proverbs 16:8

Better a little with righteousness than much gain with injustice.

Proverbs 20:7

The righteous man leads a blameless life; blessed are his children after him.

Proverbs 24:27

Finish your outdoor work and get your fields ready; after that, build your house.

Proverbs 27:1

Do not boast about tomorrow, for you do not know what a day may bring forth.

Proverbs 28:18

He whose walk is blameless is kept safe, but he whose ways are perverse will suddenly fall.

Proverbs 30:7–8

Two things I ask of you, O Lord; do not refuse me before I die: Keep falsehood and lies far from me; give me neither poverty nor riches, but give me only my daily bread.

Honesty Versus Unmerited Gain

Deuteronomy 25:15

You must have accurate and honest weights and measures, so that you may live long in the land the Lord your God is giving you.

Proverbs 11:1

The Lord abhors dishonest scales, but accurate weights are his delight.

Proverbs 16:8

Better a little with righteousness than much gain with injustice.

Proverbs 22:16

He who oppresses the poor to increase his wealth and he who gives gifts to the rich—both come to poverty.

Proverbs 28:8

He who increases his wealth by exorbitant interest amasses it for another, who will be kind to the poor.

Jeremiah 22:13

Woe to him who builds his palace by unrighteousness, his upper rooms by injustice, making his countrymen work for nothing, not paying them for their labor.

Luke 16:10

Whoever can be trusted with very little can also be trusted with much, and whoever is dishonest with very little will also be dishonest with much.

Romans 12:17

Do not repay anyone evil for evil. Be careful to do what is right in the eyes of everybody.

Humility

Proverbs 22:4

Humility and the fear of the Lord bring wealth and honor and life.

Jeremiah 9:24

"But let him who boasts boast about this: that he understands and knows me, that I am the Lord, who exercises

kindness, justice and righteousness on earth, for in these I delight," declares the Lord.

Matthew 6:1–3

"Be careful not to do your 'acts of righteousness' before men, to be seen by them. If you do, you will have no reward from your Father in heaven.

"So when you give to the needy, do not announce it with trumpets, as the hypocrites do in the synagogues and on the streets, to be honored by men. I tell you the truth, they have received their reward in full. But when you give to the needy, do not let your left hand know what your right hand is doing."

Luke 17:3

"So watch yourselves. If your brother sins, rebuke him, and if he repents, forgive him."

Luke 19:8

But Zacchaeus stood up and said to the Lord, "Look, Lord! Here and now I give half of my possessions to the poor, and if I have cheated anybody out of anything, I will pay back four times the amount."

1 Corinthians 1:26–31

Brothers, think of what you were when you were called. Not many of you were wise by human standards; not many were influential; not many were of noble birth. But God chose the foolish things of the world to shame the wise; God chose the weak things of the world to shame the strong. He chose the lowly things of this world and the despised things-and the things that are not—to nullify the things that are, so that no one may boast before him. It is because of him that you are in Christ Jesus, who has become for us wisdom from God—that is, our righteousness, holiness and redemption. Therefore, as it is written: "Let him who boasts boast in the Lord."

Inheritance

Proverbs 13:22

A good man leaves an inheritance for his children's children, but a sinner's wealth is stored up for the righteous.

Proverbs 17:2

A wise servant will rule over a disgraceful son, and will share the inheritance as one of the brothers.

Proverbs 20:21

An inheritance quickly gained at the beginning will not be blessed at the end.

Ecclesiastes 2:18–19, 21

I hated all the things I had toiled for under the sun, because I must leave them to the one who comes after me. And who knows whether he will be a wise man or a fool? Yet he will have control over all the work into which I have poured my effort and skill under the sun. This too is meaningless. For a man may do his work with wisdom, knowledge and skill, and then he must leave all he owns to someone who has not worked for it. This too is meaningless and a great misfortune.

Ezekiel 46:16–18

This is what the Sovereign Lord says: "If the prince makes a gift from his inheritance to one of his sons, it will also belong to his descendants; it is to be their property by inheritance. If, however, he makes a gift from his inheritance to one of his servants, the servant may keep it until the year of freedom; then it will revert to the prince. His inheritance belongs to his sons only; it is theirs. The prince must not take any of the inheritance of the people, driving them off their property. He is to give his sons their inheritance out of his own property, so that none of my people will be separated from his property."

Luke 15:11–31

Jesus continued: "There was a man who had two sons. The younger one said to his father, 'Father, give me my share of the estate.' So he divided his property between them.

"Not long after that, the younger son got together all he had, set off for a distant country and there squandered his wealth in wild living. After he had spent everything, there was a severe famine in that whole country, and he began to be in need. So he went and hired himself out to a citizen of that country, who sent him to his fields to feed pigs. He longed to fill his stomach with the pods that the pigs were eating, but no one gave him anything.

"When he came to his senses, he said, 'How many of my father's hired men have food to spare, and here I am starving to death! I will set out and go back to my father and say to him: Father, I have sinned against heaven and against you. I am no longer worthy to be called your son; make me like one of your hired men.' So he got up and went to his father.

"But while he was still a long way off, his father saw him and was filled with compassion for him; he ran to his son, threw his arms around him and kissed him.

"The son said to him, 'Father, I have sinned against heaven and against you. I am no longer worthy to be called your son.'

"But the father said to his servants, 'Quick! Bring the best robe and put it on him. Put a ring on his finger and sandals on his feet. Bring the fattened calf and kill it. Let's have a feast and celebrate. For this son of mine was dead and is alive again; he was lost and is found.' So they began to celebrate.

"Meanwhile, the older son was in the field. When he came near the house, he heard music and dancing. So he called one of the servants and asked him what was going on. 'Your brother has come,' he replied, 'and your father has killed the fattened calf because he has him back safe and sound.'

"The older brother became angry and refused to go in. So his father went out and pleaded with him. But he answered his father, 'Look! All these years I've been slaving for you and never disobeyed your orders. Yet you never gave me even a young goat so I could celebrate with my friends. But when this son of yours who has squandered your property with prostitutes comes home, you kill the fattened calf for him!'

"'My son,' the father said, 'you are always with me, and everything I have is yours.'"

Investing

Psalm 62:10

Do not trust in extortion or take pride in stolen goods; though your riches increase, do not set your heart on them.

Proverbs 11:24, 28

One man gives freely, yet gains even more; another withholds unduly, but comes to poverty. Whoever trusts in his riches will fall, but the righteous will thrive like a green leaf.

Proverbs 16:1–9

To man belong the plans of the heart, but from the Lord comes the reply of the tongue. All a man's ways seem innocent to him, but motives are weighed by the Lord. Commit to the Lord whatever you do, and your plans will succeed. The Lord works out everything for his own ends—even the wicked for a day of disaster. The Lord detests all the proud of heart. Be sure of this: They will not go unpunished. Through love and faithfulness sin is atoned for; through the fear of the Lord a man avoids evil. When a man's ways are pleasing to the Lord, he makes even his enemies live at peace with him. Better a little with righteousness than much gain with injustice. In his heart a man plans his course, but the Lord determines his steps.

Proverbs 21:5

The plans of the diligent lead to profit as surely as haste leads to poverty.

Proverbs 23:4–5

Do not wear yourself out to get rich; have the wisdom to show restraint. Cast but a glance at riches, and they are gone, for they will surely sprout wings and fly off to the sky like an eagle.

Investments

Proverbs 21:20

In the house of the wise are stores of choice food and oil, but a foolish man devours all he has.

Proverbs 24:27

Finish your outdoor work and get your fields ready; after that, build your house.

Ecclesiastes 6:3

A man may have a hundred children and live many years; yet no matter how long he lives, if he cannot enjoy his prosperity and does not receive proper burial, I say that a stillborn child is better off than he.

Matthew 6:19–21

"Do not store up for yourselves treasures on earth, where moth and rust destroy, and where thieves break in and steal. But store up for yourselves treasures in heaven, where moth and rust do not destroy, and where thieves do not break in and steal. For where your treasure is, there your heart will be also."

Matthew 13:22

"The one who received the seed that fell among the thorns is the man who hears the word, but the worries of this life and the deceitfulness of wealth choke it, making it unfruitful."

Matthew 25:14–30, 45

"Again, it will be like a man going on a journey, who called his servants and entrusted his property to them. To one he gave five talents of money, to another two talents, and to another one talent, each according to his ability. Then he went on his journey. The man who had received the five talents went at once and put his money to work and gained five more. So also, the one with the two talents gained two more. But the man who had received the one talent went off, dug a hole in the ground and hid his master's money.

"After a long time the master of those servants returned and settled accounts with them. The man who had received the five talents brought the other five. 'Master,' he said, 'you entrusted me with five talents. See, I have gained five more.'

"His master replied, 'Well done, good and faithful servant! You have been faithful with a few things; I will put you in charge of many things. Come and share your master's happiness!'

"The man with the two talents also came. 'Master,' he said, 'you entrusted me with two talents; see, I have gained two more.'

"His master replied, 'Well done, good and faithful servant! You have been faithful with a few things; I will put you in charge of many things. Come and share your master's happiness!'

"Then the man who had received the one talent came. 'Master,' he said, 'I knew that you are a hard man, harvesting where you have not sown and gathering where you have not scattered seed. So I was afraid and went out and hid your talent in the ground. See, here is what belongs to you.'

"His master replied, 'You wicked, lazy servant! So you knew that I harvest where I have not sown and gather where I have not scattered seed? Well then, you should

have put my money on deposit with the bankers, so that when I returned I would have received it back with interest.

"Take the talent from him and give it to the one who has the ten talents. For everyone who has will be given more, and he will have an abundance. Whoever does not have, even what he has will be taken from him. And throw that worthless servant outside, into the darkness, where there will be weeping and gnashing of teeth.' He will reply, 'I tell you the truth, whatever you did not do for one of the least of these, you did not do for me.'"

Luke 14:28–29

"Suppose one of you wants to build a tower. Will he not first sit down and estimate the cost to see if he has enough money to complete it? For if he lays the foundation and is not able to finish it, everyone who sees it will ridicule him."

Luke 19:13–26

"So he called ten of his servants and gave them ten minas. 'Put this money to work,' he said, 'until I come back.'

"But his subjects hated him and sent a delegation after him to say, 'We don't want this man to be our king.'

"He was made king, however, and returned home. Then he sent for the servants to whom he had given the money, in order to find out what they had gained with it.

"The first one came and said, 'Sir, your mina has earned ten more.'

"'Well done, my good servant!' his master replied. 'Because you have been trustworthy in a very small matter, take charge of ten cities.'

"The second came and said, 'Sir, your mina has earned five more.'

"His master answered, 'You take charge of five cities.'

"Then another servant came and said, 'Sir, here is your mina; I have kept it laid away in a piece of cloth. I was afraid of you, because you are a hard man. You take out what you did not put in and reap what you did not sow.'

"His master replied, 'I will judge you by your own words, you wicked servant! You knew, did you, that I am a hard man, taking out what I did not put in, and reaping what I did not sow? Why then didn't you put my money on deposit, so that when I came back, I could have collected it with interest?'

"Then he said to those standing by, 'Take his mina away from him and give it to the one who has ten minas.'

"'Sir,' they said, 'he already has ten!'

"He replied, 'I tell you that to everyone who has, more will be given, but as for the one who has nothing, even what he has will be taken away.'"

2 Peter 2:20

If they have escaped the corruption of the world by knowing our Lord and Savior Jesus Christ and are again entangled in it and overcome, they are worse off at the end than they were at the beginning.

2 Peter 3:10

But the day of the Lord will come like a thief. The heavens will disappear with a roar; the elements will be destroyed by fire, and the earth and everything in it will be laid bare.

Laziness

Proverbs 6:6–11

Go to the ant, you sluggard; consider its ways and be wise! It has no commander, no overseer or ruler, yet it stores its provisions in summer and gathers its food at harvest. How long will you lie there, you sluggard? When will you get up from your sleep? A little sleep, a little slumber, a little folding of the hands to rest—and poverty will come on you like a bandit and scarcity like an armed man.

Proverbs 12:24

Diligent hands will rule, but laziness ends in slave labor.

Proverbs 13:11

Dishonest money dwindles away, but he who gathers money little by little makes it grow.

Proverbs 14:4

Where there are no oxen, the manger is empty, but from the strength of an ox comes an abundant harvest.

Proverbs 19:15

Laziness brings on deep sleep, and the shiftless man goes hungry.

Proverbs 21:17

He who loves pleasure will become poor; whoever loves wine and oil will never be rich.

Proverbs 22:13

The sluggard says, "There is a lion outside!" or, "I will be murdered in the streets!"

Proverbs 26:13

The sluggard says, "There is a lion in the road, a fierce lion roaming the streets!"

2 Thessalonians 3:6, 10

In the name of the Lord Jesus Christ, we command you, brothers, to keep away from every brother who is idle and does not live according to the teaching you received from us. For even when we were with you, we gave you this rule: "If a man will not work, he shall not eat."

Lending

Exodus 22:25–26

If you lend money to one of my people among you who is needy, do not be like a moneylender; charge him no interest. If you take your neighbor's cloak as a pledge, return it to him by sunset.

Deuteronomy 23:19–20

Do not charge your brother interest, whether on money or food or anything else that may earn interest. You may charge a foreigner interest, but not a brother Israelite, so that the Lord your God may bless you in everything you put your hand to in the land you are entering to possess.

Deuteronomy 24:10–11

When you make a loan of any kind to your neighbor, do not go into his house to get what he is offering as a pledge. Stay outside and let the man to whom you are making the loan bring the pledge out to you.

Nehemiah 5:7, 10

I pondered them in my mind and then accused the nobles and officials. I told them, "You are exacting usury from your own countrymen!" So I called together a large meeting to deal with them. I and my brothers and my men are also lending the people money and grain. But let the exacting of usury stop!

Psalm 15:5

Who lends his money without usury and does not accept a bribe against the innocent. He who does these things will never be shaken.

Psalm 37:26

They are always generous and lend freely; their children will be blessed.

Proverbs 28:8

He who increases his wealth by exorbitant interest amasses it for another, who will be kind to the poor.

Ezekiel 18:8

He does not lend at usury or take excessive interest. He withholds his hand from doing wrong and judges fairly between man and man.

Luke 6:34–35

"And if you lend to those from whom you expect repayment, what credit is that to you? Even 'sinners' lend to 'sinners,' expecting to be repaid in full. But love your enemies, do good to them, and lend to them without expecting to get anything back. Then your reward will be great, and you will be sons of the Most High, because he is kind to the ungrateful and wicked."

Luke 7:41

"Two men owed money to a certain moneylender. One owed him five hundred denarii, and the other fifty."

Needs

Psalm 37:25

I was young and now I am old, yet I have never seen the righteous forsaken or their children begging bread.

Matthew 6:8, 25–33

"Do not be like them, for your Father knows what you need before you ask him.

"Therefore I tell you, do not worry about your life, what you will eat or drink; or about your body, what you will wear. Is not life more important than food, and the body more important than clothes? Look at the birds of the air; they do not sow or reap or store away in barns, and yet your heavenly Father feeds them. Are you not much more valuable than they? Who of you by worrying can add a single hour to his life?

"And why do you worry about clothes? See how the lilies of the field grow. They do not labor or spin. Yet I tell you that not even Solomon in all his splendor was dressed

like one of these. If that is how God clothes the grass of the field, which is here today and tomorrow is thrown into the fire, will he not much more clothe you, O you of little faith? So do not worry, saying, 'What shall we eat?' or 'What shall we drink?' or 'What shall we wear?' For the pagans run after all these things, and your heavenly Father knows that you need them. But seek first his kingdom and his righteousness, and all these things will be given to you as well."

Philippians 4:19

And my God will meet all your needs according to his glorious riches in Christ Jesus.

Planning

Proverbs 16:1

To man belong the plans of the heart, but from the Lord comes the reply of the tongue.

Prosperity

Genesis 39:3

When his master saw that the Lord was with him and that the Lord gave him success in everything he did.

Deuteronomy 28:11

The Lord will grant you abundant prosperity—in the fruit of your womb, the young of your livestock and the crops of your ground—in the land he swore to your forefathers to give you.

Deuteronomy 29:9

Carefully follow the terms of this covenant, so that you may prosper in everything you do.

2 Chronicles 31:21

In everything that he undertook in the service of God's temple and in obedience to the law and the commands, he sought his God and worked wholeheartedly. And so he prospered.

Psalm 1:3

He is like a tree planted by streams of water, which yields its fruit in season and whose leaf does not wither. Whatever he does prospers.

Psalm 35:27

May those who delight in my vindication shout for joy and gladness; may they always say, "The Lord be exalted, who delights in the well-being of his servant."

Luke 15:13

"Not long after that, the younger son got together all he had, set off for a distant country and there squandered his wealth in wild living."

John 6:12

When they had all had enough to eat, he said to his disciples, "Gather the pieces that are left over. Let nothing be wasted."

Retirement

Psalm 37:25

I was young and now I am old, yet I have never seen the righteous forsaken or their children begging bread.

Proverbs 16:31

Gray hair is a crown of splendor; it is attained by a righteous life.

Proverbs 20:29

The glory of young men is their strength, gray hair the splendor of the old.

Saving

Proverbs 6:6–8

Go to the ant, you sluggard; consider its ways and be wise! It has no commander, no overseer or ruler, yet it stores its provisions in summer and gathers its food at harvest.

Proverbs 21:20

In the house of the wise are stores of choice food and oil, but a foolish man devours all he has.

Proverbs 30:24–25

Four things on earth are small, yet they are extremely wise: Ants are creatures of little strength, yet they store up their food in the summer;

Sharing

Exodus 16:18–20

And when they measured it by the omer, he who gathered much did not have too much, and he who gathered little did not have too little. Each one gathered as much as he needed. Then Moses said to them, "No one is to keep any of it until morning." However, some of them paid no attention to Moses; they kept part of it until morning, but it was full of maggots and began to smell. So Moses was angry with them.

Acts 4:32

All the believers were one in heart and mind. No one claimed that any of his possessions was his own, but they shared everything they had.

Romans 12:13

Share with God's people who are in need. Practice hospitality.

1 Corinthians 9:7–11, 14

Who serves as a soldier at his own expense? Who plants a vineyard and does not eat of its grapes? Who tends a flock and does not drink of the milk? Do I say this merely from a human point of view? Doesn't the Law say the same thing? For it is written in the Law of Moses: "Do not muzzle an ox while it is treading out the grain." Is it about oxen that God is concerned? Surely he says this for us, doesn't he? Yes, this was written for us, because when the plowman plows and the thresher threshes, they ought to do so in the hope of sharing in the harvest. If we have sown spiritual seed among you, is it too much if we reap a material harvest from you? In the same way, the Lord has commanded that those who preach the gospel should receive their living from the gospel.

2 Corinthians 8:8–15

I am not commanding you, but I want to test the sincerity of your love by comparing it with the earnestness of others. For you know the grace of our Lord Jesus Christ, that though he was rich, yet for your sakes he became poor, so that you through his poverty might become rich. And here is my advice about what is best for you in this matter: Last year you were the first not only to give but also to have the desire to do so. Now finish the work, so that your eager willingness to do it may be matched by your completion of it, according to your means. For if the willingness is there, the gift is acceptable according to what one has, not according to what he does not have. Our desire is not that others might be relieved while you are hard pressed, but that there might be equality. At the present time your plenty will supply what they need, so that in turn their plenty will supply what you need. Then there will be equality, as it is written: "He who gathered much did not have too much, and he who gathered little did not have too little.

2 Corinthians 9:6–13

Remember this: Whoever sows sparingly will also reap sparingly, and whoever sows generously will also reap generously. Each man should give what he has decided in his heart to give, not reluctantly or under compulsion, for God loves a cheerful giver. And God is able to make all grace abound to you, so that in all things at all times, having all that you need, you will abound in every good work. As it is written: "He has scattered abroad his gifts to the poor; his righteousness endures forever." Now he who supplies seed to the sower and bread for food will also supply and increase your store of seed and will enlarge the harvest of your righteousness. You will be made rich in every way so that you can be generous on every occasion, and through us your generosity will result in thanksgiving to God. This service that you perform is not only supplying the needs of God's people but is also overflowing in many expressions of thanks to God. Because of the service by which you have proved yourselves, men will praise God for the obedience that accompanies your confession of the gospel of Christ, and for your generosity in sharing with them and with everyone else.

Galatians 6:6

Anyone who receives instruction in the word must share all good things with his instructor.

Self-Control

Matthew 7:13–14

Enter through the narrow gate. For wide is the gate and broad is the road that leads to destruction, and many enter through it. But small is the gate and narrow the road that leads to life, and only a few find it.

2 Corinthians 8:11

Now finish the work, so that your eager willingness to do it may be matched by your completion of it, according to your means.

Hebrews 12:11

No discipline seems pleasant at the time, but painful. Later on, however, it produces a harvest of righteousness and peace for those who have been trained by it.

Slothfulness

Proverbs 18:9

One who is slack in his work is brother to one who destroys.

Proverbs 24:30–31

I went past the field of the sluggard, past the vineyard of the man who lacks judgment; thorns had come up everywhere, the ground was covered with weeds, and the stone wall was in ruins.

Ecclesiastes 10:18

If a man is lazy, the rafters sag; if his hands are idle, the house leaks.

2 Thessalonians 3:11

We hear that some among you are idle. They are not busy; they are busybodies.

Hebrews 6:12

We do not want you to become lazy, but to imitate those who through faith and patience inherit what has been promised.

Speculation

Ecclesiastes 5:15–17

Naked a man comes from his mother's womb, and as he comes, so he departs. He takes nothing from his labor that he can carry in his hand. This too is a grievous evil: As a man comes, so he departs, and what does he gain, since he toils for the wind? All his days he eats in darkness, with great frustration, affliction and anger.

Suing

Matthew 5:42

"Give to the one who asks you, and do not turn away from the one who wants to borrow from you."

Matthew 6:3

"But when you give to the needy, do not let your left hand know what your right hand is doing."

Matthew 10:42

"And if anyone gives even a cup of cold water to one of these little ones because he is my disciple, I tell you the truth, he will certainly not lose his reward."

Matthew 13:12

"Whoever has will be given more, and he will have an abundance. Whoever does not have, even what he has will be taken from him."

Luke 6:30–36

"Give to everyone who asks you, and if anyone takes what belongs to you, do not demand it back. Do to others as you would have them do to you. "If you love those who love you, what credit is that to you? Even 'sinners'

love those who love them. And if you do good to those who are good to you, what credit is that to you? Even 'sinners' do that. And if you lend to those from whom you expect repayment, what credit is that to you? Even 'sinners' lend to 'sinners,' expecting to be repaid in full. But love your enemies, do good to them, and lend to them without expecting to get anything back. Then your reward will be great, and you will be sons of the Most High, because he is kind to the ungrateful and wicked. Be merciful, just as your Father is merciful."

Luke 12:57–58

"Why don't you judge for yourselves what is right? As you are going with your adversary to the magistrate, try hard to be reconciled to him on the way, or he may drag you off to the judge, and the judge turn you over to the officer, and the officer throw you into prison."

1 Corinthians 6:1–7

If any of you has a dispute with another, dare he take it before the ungodly for judgment instead of before the saints? Do you not know that the saints will judge the world? And if you are to judge the world, are you not competent to judge trivial cases? Do you not know that we will judge angels? How much more the things of this life! Therefore, if you have disputes about such mat-ters, appoint as judges even men of little account in the church! I say this to shame you. Is it possible that there is nobody among you wise enough to judge a dispute between believers? But instead, one brother goes to law against another-and this in front of unbelievers! The very fact that you have lawsuits among you means you have been completely defeated already. Why not rather be wronged? Why not rather be cheated?

Supporting the Wealthy

Deuteronomy 1:17

Do not show partiality in judging; hear both small and great alike. Do not be afraid of any man, for judgment belongs to God. Bring me any case too hard for you, and I will hear it.

Deuteronomy 16:19

Do not pervert justice or show partiality. Do not accept a bribe, for a bribe blinds the eyes of the wise and twists the words of the righteous.

Proverbs 14:20

But any winged creature that is clean you may eat.

Proverbs 28:21

To show partiality is not good—yet a man will do wrong for a piece of bread.

Taxes

Matthew 17:24–27

After Jesus and his disciples arrived in Capernaum, the collectors of the two-drachma tax came to Peter and asked, "Doesn't your teacher pay the temple tax?"

"Yes, he does," he replied.

When Peter came into the house, Jesus was the first to speak. "What do you think, Simon?" he asked. "From whom do the kings of the earth collect duty and taxes—from their own sons or from others?"

"From others," Peter answered. "Then the sons are exempt," Jesus said to him. "But so that we may not offend them, go to the lake and throw out your line. Take the first fish you catch; open its mouth and you will find a four-drachma coin. Take it and give it to them for my tax and yours."

Mark 12:14–17

They came to him and said, "Teacher, we know you are a man of integrity. You aren't swayed by men, because you pay no attention to who they are; but you teach the way of God in accordance with the truth. Is it right to pay taxes to Caesar or not? Should we pay or shouldn't we?" But Jesus knew their hypocrisy. "Why are you try-

ing to trap me?" he asked. "Bring me a denarius and let me look at it." They brought the coin, and he asked them, "Whose portrait is this? And whose inscription?" "Caesar's," they replied. Then Jesus said to them, "Give to Caesar what is Caesar's and to God what is God's." And they were amazed at him.

Luke 20:22–25

Is it right for us to pay taxes to Caesar or not?" He saw through their duplicity and said to them, "Show me a denarius. Whose portrait and inscription are on it?" "Caesar's," they replied. He said to them, "Then give to Caesar what is Caesar's, and to God what is God's."

Romans 13:6–7

This is also why you pay taxes, for the authorities are God's servants, who give their full time to governing. Give everyone what you owe him: If you owe taxes, pay taxes; if revenue, then revenue; if respect, then respect; if honor, then honor.

Tithing

Genesis 14:20, 22

And blessed be God Most High, who delivered your enemies into your hand." Then Abram gave him a tenth of everything. But Abram said to the king of Sodom, "I have raised my hand to the Lord, God Most High, Creator of heaven and earth, and have taken an oath."

Malachi 3:10

"Bring the whole tithe into the storehouse, that there may be food in my house. Test me in this," says the Lord Almighty, "and see if I will not throw open the floodgates of heaven and pour out so much blessing that you will not have room enough for it."

Matthew 23:23

"Woe to you, teachers of the law and Pharisees, you hypocrites! You give a tenth of your spices-mint, dill and cummin. But you have neglected the more important matters of the law-justice, mercy and faithfulness. You should have practiced the latter, without neglecting the former."

Luke 11:42

"Woe to you Pharisees, because you give God a tenth of your mint, rue and all other kinds of garden herbs, but you neglect justice and the love of God. You should have practiced the latter without leaving the former undone."

Hebrews 7:1–10

This Melchizedek was king of Salem and priest of God Most High. He met Abraham returning from the defeat of the kings and blessed him, and Abraham gave him a tenth of everything. First, his name means "king of righteousness"; then also, "king of Salem" means "king of peace." Without father or mother, without genealogy, without beginning of days or end of life, like the Son of God he remains a priest forever. Just think how great he was: Even the patriarch Abraham gave him a tenth of the plunder! Now the law requires the descendants of Levi who become priests to collect a tenth from the people-that is, their brothers-even though their brothers are descended from Abraham. This man, however, did not trace his descent from Levi, yet he collected a tenth from Abraham and blessed him who had the promises. And without doubt the lesser person is blessed by the greater. In the one case, the tenth is collected by men who die; but in the other case, by him who is declared to be living. One might even say that Levi, who collects the tenth, paid the tenth through Abraham, because when Melchizedek met Abraham, Levi was still in the body of his ancestor.

Trust

Jeremiah 17:7–8

But blessed is the man who trusts in the Lord, whose confidence is in him.

He will be like a tree planted by the water that sends out its roots by the stream. It does not fear when heat comes;

its leaves are always green. It has no worries in a year of drought and never fails to bear fruit.

Mark 6:9

Wear sandals but not an extra tunic.

Mark 8:34

Then he called the crowd to him along with his disciples and said: "If anyone would come after me, he must deny himself and take up his cross and follow me."

Philippians 4:19

And my God will meet all your needs according to his glorious riches in Christ Jesus.

Truthfulness

Psalm 1:1–2

Blessed is the man who does not walk in the counsel of the wicked or stand in the way of sinners or sit in the seat of mockers. But his delight is in the law of the Lord, and on his law he meditates day and night.

Psalm 37:37

Consider the blameless, observe the upright; there is a future for the man of peace.

Psalm 112:6

Surely he will never be shaken; a righteous man will be remembered forever.

Proverbs 10:16

The wages of the righteous bring them life, but the income of the wicked brings them punishment.

Proverbs 11:4

Wealth is worthless in the day of wrath, but righteousness delivers from death.

Proverbs 12:12

The wicked desire the plunder of evil men, but the root of the righteous flourishes.

Proverbs 13:22

A good man leaves an inheritance for his children's children, but a sinner's wealth is stored up for the righteous.

Proverbs 16:8, 11

Better a little with righteousness than much gain with injustice. Honest scales and balances are from the Lord; all the weights in the bag are of his making.

Proverbs 19:1

Better a poor man whose walk is blameless than a fool whose lips are perverse.

Proverbs 21:3

To do what is right and just is more acceptable to the Lord than sacrifice.

Proverbs 22:1

A good name is more desirable than great riches; to be esteemed is better than silver or gold.

Proverbs 28:6, 13

Better a poor man whose walk is blameless than a rich man whose ways are perverse. He who conceals his sins does not prosper, but whoever confesses and renounces them finds mercy.

Matthew 7:20

"Thus, by their fruit you will recognize them."

Matthew 17:24

After Jesus and his disciples arrived in Capernaum, the collectors of the two-drachma tax came to Peter and asked, "Doesn't your teacher pay the temple tax?"

Luke 3:12–13

Tax collectors also came to be baptized. "Teacher," they asked, "what should we do?" "Don't collect any more than you are required to," he told them.

Luke 8:15

"But the seed on good soil stands for those with a noble and good heart, who hear the word, retain it, and by persevering produce a crop."

Luke 12:58

"As you are going with your adversary to the magistrate, try hard to be reconciled to him on the way, or he may drag you off to the judge, and the judge turn you over to the officer, and the officer throw you into prison."

Romans 13:7

Give everyone what you owe him: If you owe taxes, pay taxes; if revenue, then revenue; if respect, then respect; if honor, then honor.

Romans 13:9

The commandments, "Do not commit adultery," "Do not murder," "Do not steal," "Do not covet," and whatever other commandment there may be, are summed up in this one rule: "Love your neighbor as yourself."

Galatians 6:9

Let us not become weary in doing good, for at the proper time we will reap a harvest if we do not give up.

Waste

Genesis 41:36

This food should be held in reserve for the country, to be used during the seven years of famine that will come upon Egypt, so that the country may not be ruined by the famine.

Wealth

Proverbs 10:22

Hatred stirs up dissension, but love covers over all wrongs.

Proverbs 28:13

He who conceals his sins does not prosper, but whoever confesses and renounces them finds mercy.

Jeremiah 17:8–10

He will be like a tree planted by the water that sends out its roots by the stream. It does not fear when heat comes; its leaves are always green. It has no worries in a year of drought and never fails to bear fruit." The heart is deceitful above all things and beyond cure. Who can understand it? "I the Lord search the heart and examine the mind, to reward a man according to his conduct, according to what his deeds deserve."

Luke 6:38

"Give, and it will be given to you. A good measure, pressed down, shaken together and running over, will be poured into your lap. For with the measure you use, it will be measured to you."

John 10:10

"The thief comes only to steal and kill and destroy; I have come that they may have life, and have it to the full."

2 Corinthians 8:9

For you know the grace of our Lord Jesus Christ, that though he was rich, yet for your sakes he became poor, so that you through his poverty might become rich.

Philippians 4:19

And my God will meet all your needs according to his glorious riches in Christ Jesus.

Wives

Proverbs 31:10–31

A wife of noble character who can find? She is worth far more than rubies. Her husband has full confidence in her and lacks nothing of value. She brings him good, not harm, all the days of her life. She selects wool and flax and works with eager hands. She is like the merchant ships, bringing her food from afar. She gets up while it is still dark; she provides food for her family and portions for her servant girls. She considers a field and buys it; out of her earnings she plants a vineyard. She sets about her work vigorously; her arms are strong for her tasks. She sees that her trading is profitable, and her lamp does not go out at night. In her hand she holds the distaff and grasps the spindle with her fingers. She opens her arms to the poor and extends her hands to the needy. When it snows, she has no fear for her household; for all of them are clothed in scarlet. She makes coverings for her bed; she is clothed in fine linen and purple. Her husband is respected at the city gate, where he takes his seat among the elders of the land. She makes linen garments and sells them, and supplies the merchants with sashes. She is clothed with strength and dignity; she can laugh at the days to come. She speaks with wisdom, and faithful instruction is on her tongue. She watches over the affairs of her household and does not eat the bread of idleness. Her children arise and call her blessed; her husband also, and he praises her: "Many women do noble things, but you surpass them all." Charm is deceptive, and beauty is fleeting; but a woman who fears the Lord is to be praised. Give her the reward she has earned.

Work

Deuteronomy 24:14–15

Do not take advantage of a hired man who is poor and needy, whether he is a brother Israelite or an alien living in one of your towns. Pay him his wages each day before sunset, because he is poor and is counting on it. Otherwise he may cry to the Lord against you, and you will be guilty of sin.

Proverbs 6:6–10

Go to the ant, you sluggard; consider its ways and be wise! It has no commander, no overseer or ruler, yet it stores its provisions in summer and gathers its food at harvest. How long will you lie there, you sluggard? When will you get up from your sleep? A little sleep, a little slumber, a little folding of the hands to rest.

Proverbs 10:4–5

Lazy hands make a man poor, but diligent hands bring wealth. He who gathers crops in summer is a wise son, but he who sleeps during harvest is a disgraceful son.

Proverbs 12:11, 24

He who works his land will have abundant food, but he who chases fantasies lacks judgment. Diligent hands will rule, but laziness ends in slave labor.

Proverbs 14:23

All hard work brings a profit, but mere talk leads only to poverty.

Proverbs 16:26

The laborer's appetite works for him; his hunger drives him on.

Proverbs 28:19

He who works his land will have abundant food, but the one who chases fantasies will have his fill of poverty.

Ephesians 4:28

He who has been stealing must steal no longer, but must work, doing something useful with his own hands, that he may have something to share with those in need.

Worry

Psalm 50:14–15

Sacrifice thank offerings to God, fulfill your vows to the Most High, and call upon me in the day of trouble; I will deliver you, and you will honor me.

Proverbs 12:25

An anxious heart weighs a man down, but a kind word cheers him up.

Matthew 6:27–34

"Who of you by worrying can add a single hour to his life? And why do you worry about clothes? See how the

lilies of the field grow. They do not labor or spin. Yet I tell you that not even Solomon in all his splendor was dressed like one of these. If that is how God clothes the grass of the field, which is here today and tomorrow is thrown into the fire, will he not much more clothe you, O you of little faith? So do not worry, saying, 'What shall we eat?' or 'What shall we drink?' or 'What shall we wear?' For the pagans run after all these things, and your heavenly Father knows that you need them. But seek first his kingdom and his righteousness, and all these things will be given to you as well. Therefore do not worry about tomorrow, for tomorrow will worry about itself. Each day has enough trouble of its own."

Philippians 4:6

Do not be anxious about anything, but in everything, by prayer and petition, with thanksgiving, present your requests to God.

1 John 4:18

There is no fear in love. But perfect love drives out fear, because fear has to do with punishment. The one who fears is not made perfect in love.

New International Version

Genesis 24:12

Then he prayed, "O LORD, God of my master Abraham, give me success today, and show kindness to my master Abraham.

Genesis 24:40

"He replied, 'The LORD, before whom I have walked, will send his angel with you and make your journey a success, so that you can get a wife for my son from my own clan and from my father's family.

Genesis 24:42

"When I came to the spring today, I said, 'O LORD, God of my master Abraham, if you will, please grant success to the journey on which I have come.

Genesis 24:56

But he said to them, "Do not detain me, now that the LORD has granted success to my journey. Send me on my way so I may go to my master."

Genesis 27:20

Isaac asked his son, "How did you find it so quickly, my son?" "The LORD your God gave me success," he replied.

Genesis 39:3

When his master saw that the LORD was with him and that the LORD gave him success in everything he did,

Genesis 39:23

The warden paid no attention to anything under Joseph's care, because the LORD was with Joseph and gave him success in whatever he did.

1 Samuel 18:14

In everything he did he had great success, because the LORD was with him.

1 Samuel 18:30

The Philistine commanders continued to go out to battle, and as often as they did, David met with more success than the rest of Saul's officers, and his name became well known.

1 Samuel 25:31

my master will not have on his conscience the staggering burden of needless bloodshed or of having avenged himself. And when the LORD has brought my master success, remember your servant."

1 Kings 22:13

The messenger who had gone to summon Micaiah said to him, "Look, as one man the other prophets are predicting success for the king. Let your word agree with theirs, and speak favorably."

1 Chronicles 12:18

Then the Spirit came upon Amasai, chief of the Thirty, and he said:

"We are yours, O David! We are with you, O son of Jesse! Success, success to you, and success to those who help you, for your God will help you." So David received them and made them leaders of his raiding bands.

1 Chronicles 22:11

"Now, my son, the LORD be with you, and may you have success and build the house of the LORD your God, as he said you would.

1 Chronicles 22:13

Then you will have success if you are careful to observe the decrees and laws that the LORD gave Moses for Israel. Be strong and courageous. Do not be afraid or discouraged.

2 Chronicles 18:12

The messenger who had gone to summon Micaiah said to him, "Look, as one man the other prophets are predicting success for the king. Let your word agree with theirs, and speak favorably."

2 Chronicles 26:5

He sought God during the days of Zechariah, who instructed him in the fear of God. As long as he sought the LORD, God gave him success.

Nehemiah 1:11

O Lord, let your ear be attentive to the prayer of this your servant and to the prayer of your servants who delight in revering your name. Give your servant success today by granting him favor in the presence of this man."

I was cupbearer to the king.

Nehemiah 2:20

I answered them by saying, "The God of heaven will give us success. We his servants will start rebuilding, but as for you, you have no share in Jerusalem or any claim or historic right to it."

Job 5:12

He thwarts the plans of the crafty, so that their hands achieve no success.

Job 6:13

Do I have any power to help myself, now that success has been driven from me?

Psalms 118:25

O LORD, save us; O LORD, grant us success.

Ecclesiastes 10:10

If the ax is dull and its edge unsharpened, more strength is needed but skill will bring success.

Daniel 11:14

"In those times many will rise against the king of the South. The violent men among your own people will rebel in fulfillment of the vision, but without success.

Wealth & Riches in Scripture

Wealth

Genesis 31:1

Jacob Flees from Laban: Now Jacob heard the words of Laban's sons, saying, "Jacob has taken away all that was our father's, and from what was our father's he has acquired all this wealth." (nkjv)

Genesis 34:29

And all their wealth: All their little ones and their wives they took captive; and they plundered even all that was in the houses. (nkjv)

Deuteronomy 8:17

Then you say in your heart, "My power and the might of my hand have gained me this wealth." (nkjv)

Deuteronomy 8:18

And you shall remember the Lord your God, for it is He who gives you power to get wealth, that He may establish His covenant which He swore to your fathers, as it is this day. (nkjv)

Ruth 2:1

Ruth Meets Boaz: There was a relative of Naomi's husband, a man of great wealth, of the family of Elimelech. His name was Boaz. (nkjv)

1 Kings 10:14

Solomon's Great Wealth: The weight of gold that came to Solomon yearly was six hundred and sixty-six talents of gold. (nkjv)

2 Kings 15:20

And Menahem exacted the money from Israel, from all the very wealthy, from each man fifty shekels of silver, to give to the king of Assyria. So the king of Assyria turned back, and did not stay there in the land. (nkjv)

2 Chronicles 1:11

Then God said to Solomon: "Because this was in your heart, and you have not asked riches or wealth or honor or the life of your enemies, nor have you asked long life—but have asked wisdom and knowledge for yourself, that you may judge My people over whom I have made you king." (nkjv)

2 Chronicles 1:12

Wisdom and knowledge are granted to you; and I will give you riches and wealth and honor, such as none of the kings have had who were before you, nor shall any after you have the like. (nkjv)

2 Chronicles 9:13

Solomon's Great Wealth (see also 1 Kings 10:14–29; 2 Chronicles 1:14–17): The weight of gold that came to Solomon yearly was six hundred and sixty-six talents of gold. (nkjv)

2 Chronicles 32:27

Hezekiah's Wealth and Honor (see also 2 Kings 20:12– 21; Isaiah 39:1): Hezekiah had very great riches and honor. And he made himself treasuries for silver, for gold, for precious stones, for spices, for shields, and for all kinds of desirable items. (nkjv)

Job 6:22

Did I ever say, "Bring something to me"? Or, "Offer a bribe for me from your wealth"? (nkjv)

Job 15:29

He will not be rich, nor will his wealth continue, nor will his possessions overspread the earth. (nkjv)

Job 20:10

His children will seek the favor of the poor,

And his hands will restore his wealth. (nkjv)

Job 21:13

They spend their days in wealth,

And in a moment go down to the grave. (nkjv)

Job 30:1

Job's Wealth Now Poverty: But now they mock at me, men younger than I, whose fathers I disdained to put with the dogs of my flock. (nkjv)

Job 31:25

If I have rejoiced because my wealth was great, and because my hand had gained much. (nkjv)

Psalm 49:6

Those who trust in their wealth, and boast in the multitude of their riches. (nkjv)

Psalm 49:10

For he sees wise men die; likewise the fool and the sense-less person perish, and leave their wealth to others. (nkjv)

Psalm 112:3

Wealth and riches will be in his house, and his righteousness endures forever. (nkjv)

Proverbs 5:10

Lest aliens be filled with your wealth, and your labors go to the house of a foreigner. (nkjv)

Proverbs 8:21

That I may cause those who love me to inherit wealth, that I may fill their treasuries. (nkjv)

Proverbs 10:15

The rich man's wealth is his strong city; the destruction of the poor is their poverty. (nkjv)

Proverbs 13:11

Wealth gained by dishonesty will be diminished, but he who gathers by labor will increase. (nkjv)

Proverbs 13:22

A good man leaves an inheritance to his children's children, but the wealth of the sinner is stored up for the righteous. (nkjv)

Proverbs 18:11

The rich man's wealth is his strong city, and like a high wall in his own esteem. (nkjv)

Proverbs 19:4

Wealth makes many friends, but the poor is separated from his friend. (nkjv)

Proverbs 29:3

Whoever loves wisdom makes his father rejoice, but a companion of harlots wastes his wealth. (nkjv)

Ecclesiastes 5:19

As for every man to whom God has given riches and wealth, and given him power to eat of it, to receive his heritage and rejoice in his labor—this is the gift of God. (nkjv)

Ecclesiastes 6:1

Wealth Is Not the Goal of Life: There is an evil which I have seen under the sun, and it is common among men. (nkjv)

Ecclesiastes 6:2

A man to whom God has given riches and wealth and honor, so that he lacks nothing for himself of all he desires; yet God does not give him power to eat of it, but a foreigner consumes it. This is vanity, and it is an evil affliction. (nkjv)

Song of Solomon 8:7

Many waters cannot quench love, nor can the floods drown it. If a man would give for love, all the wealth of his house, it would be utterly despised. (nkjv)

Isaiah 60:5

Then you shall see and become radiant, and your heart shall swell with joy; because the abundance of the sea shall be turned to you, the wealth of the Gentiles shall come to you. (nkjv)

Isaiah 60:11

Therefore your gates shall be open continually; they shall not be shut day or night, that men may bring to you the wealth of the Gentiles, and their kings in procession. (nkjv)

Jeremiah 15:13

Your wealth and your treasures, I will give as plunder without price, because of all your sins, throughout your territories. (nkjv)

Jeremiah 17:3

O My mountain in the field, I will give as plunder your wealth, all your treasures, and your high places of sin within all your borders. (nkjv)

Jeremiah 20:5

Moreover I will deliver all the wealth of this city, all its produce, and all its precious things; all the treasures of the kings of Judah I will give into the hand of their enemies, who will plunder them, seize them, and carry them to Babylon. (nkjv)

Ezekiel 29:19

Therefore thus says the Lord God: "Surely I will give the land of Egypt to Nebuchadnezzar king of Babylon; he shall take away her wealth, carry off her spoil, and remove her pillage; and that will be the wages for his army." (nkjv)

Ezekiel 30:4

The sword shall come upon Egypt, and great anguish shall be in Ethiopia, when the slain fall in Egypt, and they take away her wealth, and her foundations are broken down. (nkjv)

Hosea 12:8

And Ephraim said, "Surely I have become rich, I have found wealth for myself; In all my labors, they shall find in me no iniquity that is sin." (nkjv)

Nahum 2:9

Take spoil of silver! Take spoil of gold! There is no end of treasure, or wealth of every desirable prize. (nkjv)

Zechariah 14:14

Judah also will fight at Jerusalem. And the wealth of all the surrounding nations shall be gathered together: Gold, silver, and apparel in great abundance. (nkjv)

Revelation 3:17

Because you say, "I am rich, have become wealthy, and have need of nothing"—and do not know that you are wretched, miserable, poor, blind, and naked. (nkjv)

Revelation 18:19

They threw dust on their heads and cried out, weeping and wailing, and saying, "Alas, alas, that great city, in which all who had ships on the sea became rich by her wealth! For in one hour she is made desolate." (nkjv)

Rich and Riches

Genesis 13:2

Abram was very rich in livestock, in silver, and in gold. (nkjv)

Genesis 14:23

That I will take nothing, from a thread to a sandal strap, and that I will not take anything that is yours, lest you should say, "I have made Abram rich." (nkjv)

Genesis 49:20

Bread from Asher shall be rich, and he shall yield royal dainties. (nkjv)

Exodus 30:15

The rich shall not give more and the poor shall not give less than half a shekel, when you give an offering to the Lord, to make atonement for yourselves. (nkjv)

Leviticus 25:47

Now if a sojourner or stranger close to you becomes rich, and one of your brethren who dwells by him becomes poor, and sells himself to the stranger or sojourner close to you, or to a member of the stranger's family. (nkjv)

Numbers 13:20

Whether the land is rich or poor; and whether there are forests there or not. Be of good courage. And bring some of the fruit of the land. (nkjv)

Ruth 3:10

Then he said, "Blessed are you of the Lord, my daughter! For you have shown more kindness at the end than at the beginning, in that you did not go after young men, whether poor or rich." (nkjv)

1 Samuel 2:7

The Lord makes poor and makes rich; He brings low and lifts up. (nkjv)

1 Samuel 25:2

Now there was a man in Maon whose business was in Carmel, and the man was very rich. He had three thousand sheep and a thousand goats. And he was shearing his sheep in Carmel. (nkjv)

2 Samuel 12:1

Then the Lord sent Nathan to David. And he came to him, and said to him: "There were two men in one city, one rich and the other poor." (nkjv)

2 Samuel 12:2

The rich man had exceedingly many flocks and herds. (nkjv)

2 Samuel 12:4

And a traveler came to the rich man, who refused to take from his own flock and from his own herd to prepare one for the wayfaring man who had come to him; but he took the poor man's lamb and prepared it for the man who had come to him. (nkjv)

2 Samuel 19:32

Now Barzillai was a very aged man, eighty years old. And he had provided the king with supplies while he stayed at Mahanaim, for he was a very rich man. (nkjv)

1 Chronicles 4:40

And they found rich, good pasture, and the land was broad, quiet, and peaceful; for some Hamites formerly lived there. (nkjv)

Nehemiah 9:25

And they took strong cities and a rich land, and possessed houses full of all goods, cisterns already dug, vineyards, olive groves, and fruit trees in abundance. So they ate and were filled and grew fat,

And delighted themselves in your great goodness. (nkjv)

Nehemiah 9:35

For they have not served You in their kingdom, or in the many good things that you gave them, or in the large and rich land which You set before them; nor did they turn from their wicked works. (nkjv)

Job 15:29

He will not be rich, nor will his wealth continue, nor will his possessions overspread the earth. (nkjv)

Job 27:19

The rich man will lie down, but not be gathered up; he opens his eyes, and he is no more. (nkjv)

Job 34:19

Yet He is not partial to princes, nor does He regard the rich more than the poor; for they are all the work of His hands. (nkjv)

Psalm 45:12

And the daughter of Tyre will come with a gift; the rich among the people will seek your favor. (nkjv)

Psalm 49:2

Both low and high, rich and poor together. (nkjv)

Psalm 49:16

Do not be afraid when one becomes rich, when the glory of his house is increased. (nkjv)

Psalm 66:12

You have caused men to ride over our heads; we went through fire and through water; but You brought us out to rich fulfillment. (nkjv)

Proverbs 10:4

He who has a slack hand becomes poor, but the hand of the diligent makes rich. (nkjv)

Proverbs 10:22

The blessing of the Lord makes one rich, and He adds no sorrow with it. (nkjv)

Proverbs 11:25

The generous soul will be made rich, and he who waters will also be watered himself. (nkjv)

Proverbs 13:4

The soul of a lazy man desires, and has nothing; but the soul of the diligent shall be made rich. (nkjv)

Proverbs 13:7

There is one who makes himself rich, yet has nothing; and one who makes himself poor, yet has great riches. (nkjv)

Proverbs 14:20

The poor man is hated even by his own neighbor, but the rich has many friends. (nkjv)

Proverbs 18:23

The poor man uses entreaties, but the rich answers roughly. (nkjv)

Proverbs 21:17

He who loves pleasure will be a poor man; he who loves wine and oil will not be rich. (nkjv)

Proverbs 22:2

The rich and the poor have this in common, the Lord is the maker of them all. (nkjv)

Proverbs 22:7

The rich rules over the poor, and the borrower is servant to the lender. (nkjv)

Proverbs 22:16

He who oppresses the poor to increase his riches, and he who gives to the rich, will surely come to poverty. (nkjv)

Colossians 1:27

To them God willed to make known what are the riches of the glory of this mystery among the Gentiles: which is Christ in you, the hope of glory. (nkjv)

Colossians 2:2

That their hearts may be encouraged, being knit together in love, and attaining to all riches of the full assurance of understanding, to the knowledge of the mystery of God, both of the Father and of Christ. (nkjv)

1 Timothy 6:17

Command those who are rich in this present age not to be haughty, nor to trust in uncertain riches but in the living God, who gives us richly all things to enjoy. (nkjv)

Hebrews 11:26

Esteeming the reproach of Christ greater riches than the treasures in Egypt; for he looked to the reward. (nkjv)

James 5:2

Your riches are corrupted, and your garments are moth-eaten. (nkjv)

Revelation 5:12

Saying with a loud voice: "Worthy is the Lamb who was slain To receive power and riches and wisdom, And strength and honor and glory and blessing!" (nkjv)

Revelation 18:17

*"For in one hour such great riches came to nothing."
Every shipmaster, all who travel by ship, sailors, and as
many as trade on the sea, stood at a distance. (nkjv)*

Source Material

21 Unbreakable Laws of Success, Max Anders, Thomas Nelson, 1996

A Christian Guide to Prosperity; Fries & Taylor, California: Communications Research, 1984

A Look At Stewardship, Word Aflame Publications, 2001

American Savings Education Council (http://www.asec.org)

Anointed For Business, Ed Silvoso, Regal, 2002

Avoiding Common Financial Mistakes, Ron Blue, Navpress, 1991

Baker Encyclopedia of the Bible; Walter Elwell, Michigan: Baker Book House, 1988

Becoming The Best, Barry Popplewell, England: Gower Publishing Company Limited, 1988

Business Proverbs, Steve Marr, Fleming H. Revell, 2001

Cheapskate Monthly, Mary Hunt

Commentary on the Old Testament; Keil-Delitzsch, Michigan: Eerdmans Publishing, 1986

Crown Financial Ministries, various publications

Customers As Partners, Chip Bell, Texas: Berrett-Koehler Publishers, 1994

Cut Your Bills in Half; Pennsylvania: Rodale Press, Inc., 1989

Debt-Free Living, Larry Burkett, Dimensions, 2001

Die Broke, Stephen M. Pollan & Mark Levine, HarperBusiness, 1997

Double Your Profits, Bob Fifer, Virginia: Lincoln Hall Press, 1993

Eerdmans' Handbook to the Bible, Michigan: William B. Eerdmans Publishing Company, 1987

Eight Steps to Seven Figures, Charles B. Carlson, Double Day, 2000

Everyday Life in Bible Times; Washington DC: National Geographic Society, 1967

Financial Dominion, Norvel Hayes, Harrison House, 1986

Financial Freedom, Larry Burkett, Moody Press, 1991

Financial Freedom, Patrick Clements, VMI Publishers, 2003

Financial Peace, Dave Ramsey, Viking Press, 2003

Financial Self-Defense; Charles Givens, New York: Simon And Schuster, 1990

Flood Stage, Oral Roberts, 1981

Generous Living, Ron Blue, Zondervan, 1997

Get It All Done, Tony and Robbie Fanning, New York:Pennsylvania: Chilton Book, 1979

Getting Out of Debt, Howard Dayton, Tyndale House, 1986

Getting Out of Debt, Mary Stephenson, Fact Sheet 436, University of Maryland Cooperative Extension Service, 1988

Giving and Tithing, Larry Burkett, Moody Press, 1991

God's Plan For Giving, John MacArthur, Jr., Moody Press, 1985

God's Will is Prosperity, Gloria Copeland, Harrison House, 1978

Great People of the Bible and How They Lived; New York: Reader's Digest, 1974

How Others Can Help You Get Out of Debt; Esther M. Maddux, Circular 759-3,

How To Make A Business Plan That Works, Henderson, North Island Sound Limited, 1989

How To Manage Your Money, Larry Burkett, Moody Press, 1999

How to Personally Profit From the Laws of Success, Sterling Sill, NIFP, Inc., 1978

How to Plan for Your Retirement; New York: Corrigan & Kaufman, Longmeadow Press, 1985

Is God Your Source?, Oral Roberts, 1992

It's Not Luck, Eliyahu Goldratt, Great Barrington, MA: The North River Press, 1994

Jesus CEO, Laurie Beth Jones, Hyperion, 1995

John Avanzini Answers Your Questions About Biblical Economics, Harrison House, 1992

Living on Less and Liking It More, Maxine Hancock, Chicago, Illinois: Moody Press, 1976

Making It Happen; Charles Conn, New Jersey: Fleming H. Revell Company, 1981

Master Your Money Or It Will Master You, Arlo E. Moehlenpah, Doing Good Ministries, 1999

Master Your Money; Ron Blue, Tennessee: Thomas Nelson, Inc. 1986

Miracle of Seed Faith, Oral Roberts, 1970

Mississippi State University Extension Service

Money, Possessions, and Eternity, Randy Alcorn, Tyndale House, 2003

More Than Enough, David Ramsey, Penguin Putnam Inc, 2002

Moving the Hand of God, John Avanzini, Harrison House, 1990

Multiplication, Tommy Barnett, Creation House, 1997

NebFacts, Nebraska Cooperative Extension

New York Post

One Up On Wall Street; New York: Peter Lynch, Simon And Schuster, 1989

Personal Finances, Larry Burkett, Moody Press, 1991

Portable MBA in Finance and Accounting; Livingstone, Canada: John Wiley & Sons, Inc., 1992

Principle-Centered Leadership, Stephen R. Covey, New York: Summit Books, 1991

Principles of Financial Management, Kolb & DeMong, Texas: Business Publications, Inc., 1988

Rapid Debt Reduction Strategies, John Avanzini, HIS Publishing, 1990

Real Wealth, Wade Cook, Arizona: Regency Books, 1985

See You At The Top, Zig Ziglar, Louisianna: Pelican Publishing Company, 1977

Seed-Faith Commentary on the Holy Bible, Oral Roberts, Pinoak Publications, 1975

Sharkproof, Harvey Mackay, New York: HarperCollins Publishers, 1993

Smart Money, Ken and Daria Dolan, New York: Random House, Inc., 1988

Strong's Concordance, Tennessee: Crusade Bible Publishers, Inc.,

Success by Design, Peter Hirsch, Bethany House, 2002

Success is the Quality of your Journey, Jennifer James, New York: Newmarket Press, 1983

Swim with the Sharks Without Being Eaten Alive, Harvey Mackay, William Morrow , 1988

The Almighty and the Dollar; Jim McKeever, Oregon: Omega Publications, 1981

The Challenge, Robert Allen, New York: Simon And Schuster, 1987

The Family Financial Workbook, Larry Burkett, Moody Press, 2002

The Management Methods of Jesus, Bob Briner, Thomas Nelson, 1996

The Millionaire Next Door, Thomas Stanley & William Danko, Pocket Books, 1996

The Money Book for Kids, Nancy Burgeson, Troll Associates,1992

The Money Book for King's Kids; Harold E. Hill, New Jersey: Fleming H. Revell Company, 1984

The Seven Habits of Highly Effective People, Stephen Covey, New York: Simon And Schuster, 1989

The Wealthy Barber, David Chilton, California: Prima Publishing, 1991

Theological Wordbook of the Old Testament, Chicago, Illinois: Moody Press, 1981

Treasury of Courage and Confidence, Norman Vincent Peale, New York: Doubleday & Co., 1970

True Prosperity, Dick Iverson, Bible Temple Publishing, 1993

Trust God For Your Finances, Jack Hartman, Lamplight Publications, 1983

University of Georgia Cooperative Extension Service, 1985

Virginia Cooperative Extension

Webster's Unabridged Dictionary, Dorset & Baber, 1983

What Is an Entrepreneur; David Robinson, MA: Kogan Page Limited, 1990

Word Meanings in the New Testament, Ralph Earle, Michigan: Baker Book House, 1986

Word Pictures in the New Testament; Robertson, Michigan: Baker Book House, 1930

Word Studies in the New Testament; Vincent, New York: Charles Scribner's Sons, 1914

Worth

You Can Be Financially Free, George Fooshee, Jr., 1976, Fleming H. Revell Company.

Your Key to God's Bank, Rex Humbard, 1977

Your Money Counts, Howard, Dayton, Tyndale House, 1997

Your Money Management, MaryAnn Paynter, Circular 1271, University of Illinois Cooperative Extension Service, 1987.

Your Money Matters, Malcolm MacGregor, Bethany Fellowship, Inc., 1977

Your Road to Recovery, Oral Roberts, Oliver Nelson, 1986

Comments On Sources

Over the years I have collected bits and pieces of interesting material, written notes on sermons I've heard, jotted down comments on financial articles I've read, and gathered a lot of great information. It is unfortunate that I didn't record the sources of all of these notes in my earlier years. I gratefully extend my appreciation to the many writers, authors, teachers and pastors from whose articles and sermons I have gleaned much insight.

Rich Brott

Online Resources

American Savings Education Council (http://www.asec.org)

Bloomberg.com (http://www.bloomberg.com)

Bureau of the Public Debt Online (http://www.publicdebt.treas.gov)

BusinessWeek (http://www.businessweek.com)

Charles Schwab & Co., Inc. (http://www.schwab.com)

Consumer Federation of America (http://www.consumerfed.org)

Debt Advice.org (http://www.debtadvice.org)

Federal Reserve System (http://www.federalreserve.gov)

Fidelity Investments (http://www.fidelity.com)

Financial Planning Association (http://www.fpanet.org)

Forbes (www.forbes.com)

Fortune Magazine (http://www.fortune.com)

Generous Giving (http://www.generousgiving.org/)

Investing for Your Future (http://www.investing.rutgers.edu)

Kiplinger Magazine (http://www.kiplinger.com/)

Money Magazine (http://money.cnn.com)

MorningStar (http://www.morningstar.com)

MSN Money (http://moneycentral.msn.com)

Muriel Siebert (http://www.siebertnet.com)

National Center on Education and the Economy (http://www.ncee.org)

National Foundation for Credit Counseling (http://www.nfcc.org)

Quicken (http://www.quicken.com)

Smart Money (http://www.smartmoney.com)

Social Security Online (http://www.ssa.gov)

Standard & Poor's (http://www2.standardandpoors.com)

The Dollar Stretcher, Gary Foreman, (http://www.stretcher.com)

The Vanguard Group (http://flagship.vanguard.com)

U.S. Securities and Exchange Commission (http://www.sec.gov)

Yahoo! Finance (http://finance.yahoo.com)

Magazine Resources

Business Week
Consumer Reports
Forbes
Kiplinger's Personal Finance
Money
Smart Money
US News and World Report

Newspaper Resources

Barrons

Investors Business Daily

USA Today

Wall Street Journal

Washington Times

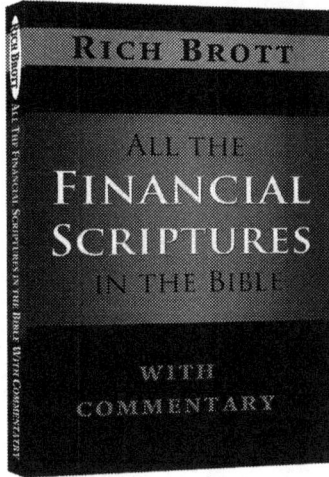

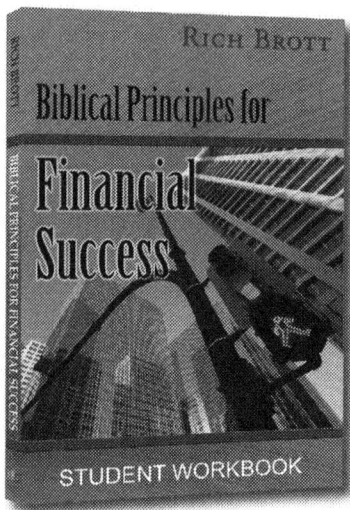

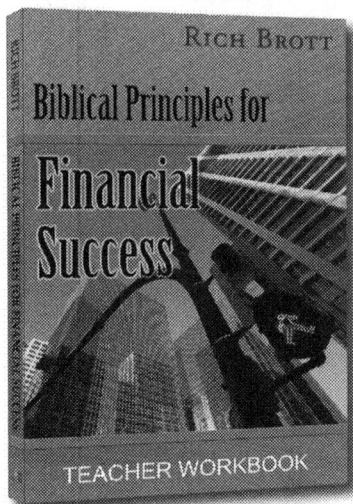